Practitioner Resource Guide: The Psychology of Financial Planning

Certified Financial Planner Board of Standards, Inc.

ISBN: 978-1-954096-90-5

Certified Financial Planner Board of Standards, Inc.
1425 K Street NW #800
Washington, D.C. 20005

Printed in the United States of America

Cover art by Maria/Adobe Stock

TABLE OF CONTENTS

PREFACE

Comprehensive, fiduciary financial planning is so much more than being competent at financial planning technical skills. You may be able to develop the most complex tax planning projections at your firm or develop detailed strategies to maximize income from the sale of stock options; these skills are valuable to your clients and are essential functions of being a CERTIFIED FINANCIAL PLANNER™ professional. But, in order to maximize your value to clients, you must also be able to communicate effectively and deliver recommendations in a way that moves client motivation forward through recommendation implementation (in addition to many other skills discussed in detail in this book).

The psychology of financial planning is CFP Board's newest financial planning domain. CFP Board defines the Psychology of Financial Planning as "**identifying and responding to attitudes, behaviors, and situations that impact decision-making, the client-planner relationship, and the client's financial well-being**." Within the Psychology of Financial Planning domain, client characteristics and financial planner characteristics intersect. It can be described as the "the system within which clients planning for their financial goals and financial well-being are aided by financial planners who possess their own history, biases and values that must be recognized and sometimes subsumed in service to the client" (CFP Board, n.d.).

This book is written by financial planning practitioners for financial planning practitioners. It is intended to complement *The Psychology of Financial Planning* by providing CERTIFIED FINANCIAL PLANNER™ professionals with resources and tools to incorporate the psychology of financial planning into their practice. To put it another way, this book was written to provide financial planners with the resources to take the concepts and information described in *The Psychology of Financial Planning* and implement this information in work with clients. *The Psychology of Financial Planning* provides the *what*; this Practitioner's Resource Guide provides the *how*. As such, this book addresses every Principal Knowledge Topic for the Psychology of Financial Planning domain and is laid out in 15 chapters parallel to *The Psychology of Financial Planning*. These

1. Client and planner attitudes, values, and biases

2. Behavioral finance

3. Sources of money conflict

4. Principles of counseling

5. General principles of effective communication

6. Crisis events with severe consequences

In keeping the needs of practitioners at the forefront of this book's design, this book is comprised of step-by-step guides, do's and don'ts lists, exercises, assessments, examples and other helpful figures and lists to highlight what you need to know and how to apply the information.

The authors of this book recommend reading *The Psychology of Financial Planning* prior to reading this companion guide although the most salient points from each chapter from *The Psychology of Financial Planning* are briefly summarized to provide a foundation for the new content. Some readers may find it most useful to read the entirety of The Psychology of Financial Planning prior to reading this companion guide. Others may prefer to read Chapter 1 of this work directly after reading the first chapter of The Psychology of Financial Planning, and then proceeding on to the second chapters of each book.

One of the most valuable resources this book provides is the list of books, blog posts, research articles, and websites listed in the reference list of each chapter. The resources cited in this book were selected carefully, to be as useful and practical to financial planners as possible. This approach is truly what makes this book a "Practitioner's Resource Guide."

REFERENCES

CFP Board. (n.d.). *The psychology of financial planning.* https://www.cfp.net/knowledge/psychology-of-financial-planning.

Chapter 1

Framing Advice in Light of Client's Risk Tolerance

1.1 INTRODUCTION

Risk tolerance is most widely defined as the maximum amount of uncertainty a person is willing to accept when making a financial decision (Grable, 2000). In other words, you can think of risk tolerance as a person's willingness to take risk. However, risk tolerance is multifaceted, and can be conceptualized differently. For this reason, this chapter will define a number of different terms related to financial risk tolerance to illustrate the complexity of a client's risk tolerance. Another contributing factor that can make risk tolerance difficult to account for is that risk tolerance is individual. If you are working with a couple or doing multigenerational planning, each person in the planning engagement has their own willingness to tolerate uncertainty. Planners must be able to address and account for the differences in risk tolerance. The larger the differences in each person's risk tolerance, the more difficult this becomes. This chapter will provide you with a foundational understanding of what risk tolerance is and how you can measure it. You will also understand how your client's risk tolerance may impact their behavior.

1.2 RISK TOLERANCE CONSIDERATIONS IN PRACTICE

In practice, risk tolerance is typically measured for compliance and regulatory purposes and is used to choose a portfolio allocation for clients. The typical assumption is that clients with a higher risk tolerance are able to stomach more volatility in their

> **Risk Tolerance**
>
> Risk tolerance is the maximum amount of uncertainty that a person is willing to accept when making a financial decision.

portfolio. Theoretically, these clients will be able to take advantage of the higher potential for returns over the long-term by taking more risk with their investment mix. Of course, they will, in all likelihood, face more severe losses in their portfolios than clients who are invested more conservatively when the financial markets are in turmoil. These potential large portfolio losses can be very difficult to stomach. From a fiduciary perspective, it is essential to ensure that clients are not invested in portfolios that are too risky for their risk appetite that may result in greater losses than they can stomach. It is rarely in a client's best interests to move to a more conservative portfolio or move all to cash in a down market.

Although risk tolerance and investment recommendations will always be closely related, it is important for financial planning practitioners to understand that risk tolerance impacts clients' other financial decisions and behaviors too. For example, your clients' risk tolerance may impact their decisions related to debt payoff or annuitizing some of their assets. Clients with a low risk tolerance may strongly prefer to pay off a low interest mortgage with funds from their investment portfolio even when their investments have a higher long-term expected rate of return. The same clients may also strongly prefer to use the funds in their brokerage account to purchase an annuity given the perceived safety of a lifetime income stream over the volatility of the stock and bond market. You may have greater success with clients implementing recommendations if you understand how to frame your advice in light of a client's risk tolerance.

The bullet points listed here summarize points from Chapter 1: Framing Advice in Light of Client's Risk Tolerance in *The Psychology of Financial Planning* (Chatterjee and Yeske, 2022). This list highlights important concepts that are particularly relevant for financial planning practitioners to incorporate in their work with clients.

- Risk tolerance is an important actor, not only for investment decisions, but also for many other types of financial decisions and preferences.

- There are many ways to measure risk tolerance. The primary methods include professional judgement, heuristics, risk tolerance scales, and triangulation. Each method has its own pros and cons.

- Your role as a financial planner is to help your clients arrive at decisions that correspond with their values but are also financially wise and consistent with their risk tolerance and good quality financial advice.

1.3 RISK TOLERANCE TERMS

Each of the important risk tolerance terms in this chapter are identified and defined below in Figure 1.1. Understand that risk tolerance is multifaceted and complex. Clients with a generally high risk tolerance may also have a risk preference or a risk attitude in a specific situation or in light of a certain goal that causes them to act inconsistently with someone generally comfortable with uncertainty. Additionally, many financial advisors have been frustrated by clients who have a large risk capacity but a low financial risk tolerance and want to be invested primarily in cash and bonds. Once you understand the various risk tolerance factors at play in a situation, you can work with your clients to help them increase their risk literacy and reach the optimal outcomes.

Figure 1.1. Risk Tolerance Terms

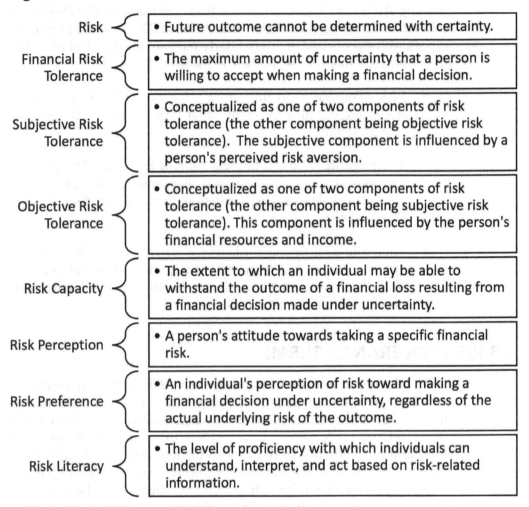

Risk	• Future outcome cannot be determined with certainty.
Financial Risk Tolerance	• The maximum amount of uncertainty that a person is willing to accept when making a financial decision.
Subjective Risk Tolerance	• Conceptualized as one of two components of risk tolerance (the other component being objective risk tolerance). The subjective component is influenced by a person's perceived risk aversion.
Objective Risk Tolerance	• Conceptualized as one of two components of risk tolerance (the other component being subjective risk tolerance). This component is influenced by the person's financial resources and income.
Risk Capacity	• The extent to which an individual may be able to withstand the outcome of a financial loss resulting from a financial decision made under uncertainty.
Risk Perception	• A person's attitude towards taking a specific financial risk.
Risk Preference	• An individual's perception of risk toward making a financial decision under uncertainty, regardless of the actual underlying risk of the outcome.
Risk Literacy	• The level of proficiency with which individuals can understand, interpret, and act based on risk-related information.

1.4 MEASURING RISK TOLERANCE

There are several different ways to measure subjective risk tolerance. Figure 1.2 includes a list of ways risk tolerance can be measured in practice. Bear in mind that none of these measures are perfect. There is a lack of consensus in the academic and practitioner communities regarding the best way to measure risk tolerance. Identifying and understanding how to measure risk tolerance most accurately and effectively in practice is an area where much work remains to be done.

Figure 1.2. Measuring Subjective Risk Tolerance

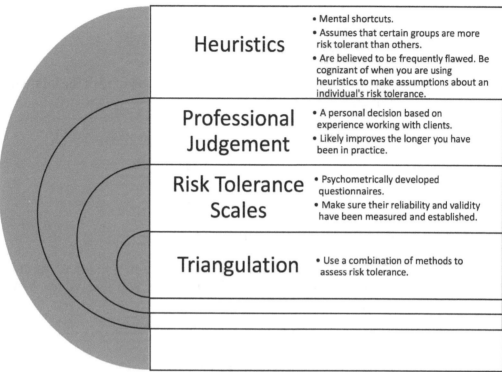

John Grable and Ruth Lytton (1999) developed a psychometrically validated risk tolerance scale that has been widely used in research. In all likelihood, your firm already has a preferred system in place for assessing risk tolerance. However, if you have not yet assessed your own risk tolerance, it is time to do so. The recommendations you make to your clients may be impacted by your own risk tolerance. In light of this, it is important to understand your own risk tolerance so that you can be aware of how it may impact your recommendations. You may wish to take multiple assessments to ensure the results are consistent. The questionnaire below could be a good starting point for understanding your own risk tolerance.

Grable-Lytton (GL) Risk-Tolerance Scale

1. In general, how would your best friend describe you as a risk taker?

    b. Willing to take risks after completing adequate research

    c. Cautious

    d. A real risk avoider

2. You are on a TV game show and can choose one of the following. Which would you take?

    a. $1,000 in cash

    b. A 50% chance at winning $5,000

    c. A 25% chance at winning $10,000

    d. A 5% chance at winning $100,000

3. You have just finished saving for a "once-in-a-lifetime" vacation. Three weeks before you plan to leave, you lose your job. You would:

    a. Cancel the vacation

    b. Take a much more modest vacation

    c. Go as scheduled, reasoning that you need the time to prepare for a job search

    d. Extend your vacation, because this might be your last chance to go first-class

4. If you unexpectedly received $20,000 to invest, what would you do?

    a. Deposit it in a bank account, money market account, or an insured CD

    b. Invest it in safe high-quality bonds or bond mutual funds

    c. Invest it in stocks or stock mutual funds

5. In terms of experience, how comfortable are you investing in stocks or stock mutual funds?

    a. Not at all comfortable

    b. Somewhat comfortable

    c. Very comfortable

6. When you think of the word "risk" which of the following words comes to mind first?

    a. Loss

    b. Uncertainty

    c. Opportunity

    d. Thrill

7. Some experts are predicting prices of assets such as gold, jewels, collectibles, and real estate (hard assets) to increase in value; bond prices may fall, however, experts tend to agree that government bonds are relatively safe. Most of your investment assets are now in high interest government bonds. What would you do?

    a. Hold the bonds

    b. Sell the bonds, put half the proceeds into money market accounts, and the other half into hard assets

    c. Sell the bonds and put the total proceeds into hard assets

    d. Sell the bonds, put all the money into hard assets, and borrow additional money to buy more

8. Given the best and worst case returns of the four investment choices below, which would you prefer?

    a. $200 gain best case; $0 gain/loss worst case

    b. $800 gain best case; $200 loss worst case

    c. $2,600 gain best case; $800 loss worst case

    d. $4,800 gain best case; $2,400 loss worst case

9. In addition to whatever you own, you have been given $1,000. You are now asked to choose between:

    a. A sure gain of $500

    b. A 50% chance to gain $1,000 and a 50% chance to gain nothing

10. In addition to whatever you own, you have been given $2,000. You are now asked to choose between:

    a. A sure loss of $500

    b. A 50% chance to lose $1,000 and a 50% chance to lose nothing

11. Suppose a relative left you an inheritance of $100,000, stipulating in the will that you invest ALL the money in ONE of the following choices. Which one would you select?

    a. A savings account or money market mutual fund

    b. A mutual fund that owns stocks and bonds

    c. A portfolio of 15 common stocks

    d. Commodities like gold, silver, and oil

12. If you had to invest $20,000, which of the following investment choices would you find most appealing?

    a. 60% in low-risk investments 30% in medium-risk investments 10% in high-risk investments

    b. 30% in low-risk investments 40% in medium-risk investments 30% in high-risk investments

    c. 10% in low-risk investments 40% in medium-risk investments

13. Your trusted friend and neighbor, an experienced geologist, is putting together a group of investors to fund an exploratory gold mining venture. The venture could pay back 50 to 100 times the investment if successful. If the mine is a bust, the entire investment is worthless. Your friend estimates the chance of success is only 20%. If you had the money, how much would you invest?

   a. Nothing

   b. One month's salary

   c. Three month's salary

   d. Six month's salary

Scoring

1. a=4; b=3; c=2; d=1   **Your Answer_____**

2. a=1; b=2; c=3; d=4   **Your Answer_____**

3. a=1; b=2; c=3; d=4   **Your Answer_____**

4. a=1; b=2; c=3   **Your Answer_____**

5. a=1; b=2; c=3   **Your Answer_____**

6. a=1; b=2; c=3; d=4   **Your Answer_____**

7. a=1; b=2; c=3; d=4   **Your Answer_____**

8. a=1; b=2; c=3; d=4   **Your Answer_____**

9. a=1; b=3   **Your Answer_____**

10. a=1; b=3   **Your Answer_____**

11. a=1; b=2; c=3; d=4   **Your Answer_____**

12. a=1; b=2; c=3   **Your Answer_____**

13. a=1; b=2; c=3; d=4   **Your Answer_____**

The lowest score achievable on this assessment is a 13 while the highest possible score is a 47. Understanding where you score in this range will give you a sense of how high or low your risk tolerance is.

Now that you've assessed your own risk tolerance, it is time to consider how this may impact the financial recommendations you make to your clients. It may also be worthwhile considering the tools you have been using to assess your clients' risk tolerance. Are you using multiple methods of measuring risk tolerance or just one? Has the assessment you are using been tested for reliability and validity? In other words, has the assessment been shown to be consistent (i.e., reliable) and evaluated to determine if it measures the variable that it is intended to (i.e., valid) (Jhangiani et al., 2019). If a large number of your clients are moving or wanting to move to more conservative portfolios during market downturns, you may need to reevaluate your risk tolerance assessment and portfolio allocation methodologies and processes.

1.5 FACTORS THAT IMPACT RISK TOLERANCE

Research shows that there are some characteristics that are associated with having a higher or a lower risk tolerance. Although risk tolerance cannot purely be predicted by these factors, it may be helpful as you work to develop a general understanding of your client's risk profile and their willingness to tolerate uncertainty. Figure 1.3 describes some of these factors. This may also be useful in understanding how, as some of these factors may change over time, your client's risk profile may change as well.

Some of the factors described below in Figure 1.3 need additional research as results have been mixed. One of the areas that needs additional research is understanding the relationship between risk tolerance and race/ethnic groups. Research generally indicates that white respondents typically have a higher risk tolerance than Blacks and Hispanics. However, some of these differences should likely be attributed to systemic problems that have impacted levels of education, wealth, and income more than socialization and culture.

Figure 1.3. Lower and Higher Risk Tolerance Factors

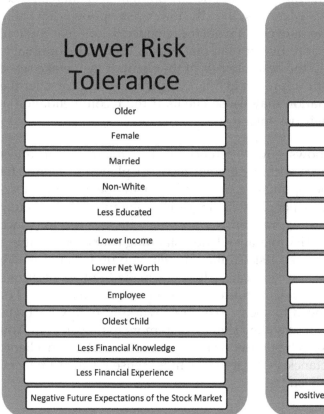
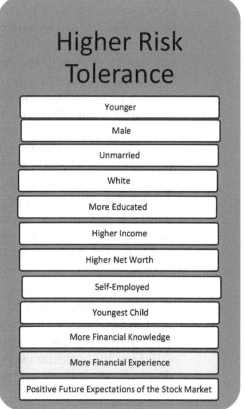

1.6 THE IMPACT OF RISK TOLERANCE ON FINANCIAL DECISIONS

Although risk tolerance is widely used in practice for asset allocation and investment decisions, it is infrequently considered in the context of other financial behaviors. Figure 1.4 illustrates how clients' risk tolerance may impact their preferences for different financial decisions. In all likelihood, you have at some point been frustrated by clients who did not follow through on a recommendation. You lay out the options and discuss the financially optimal choice, yet after your clients discuss and acknowledge that they appreciate your advice, they decide to make a different decision.

Clients with a low-risk tolerance may prefer a safer or more "guaranteed" option, even if the outcome is not financially optimal. If clients can meet their goals while taking less risk, then the lower risk option is likely the best option for the clients even if it is not the "financially optimal" option. It may seem counterintuitive at first, but what is financially optimal is not always what is in the best interests of the client. It may make sense to take a more holistic approach to financial planning and consider the stress a recommendation may cause clients if the recommendation is inconsistent with their risk tolerance.

Figure 1.4 below shows how differences in risk tolerance can affect a person's preferences within different areas of planning. Figure 1.4 is *not* indicating the optimal recommendation for people with low-risk tolerances versus people with high-risk tolerances. It is merely summarizing the natural preferences of people with low-risk tolerance and people with high-risk tolerance. Understanding your clients' natural preferences based on their risk profile can help you understand where they are and decide how you can help them make the best decisions regarding debt management, retirement income, and insurance. For example, you may need to spend extra time working with your high-risk tolerant clients on why they should keep more money in cash. You may also need to take extra time educating your low-risk tolerant clients with long life expectancies why it makes more sense for their financial plan to delay Social Security.

Figure 1.4. How Differences in Risk Tolerance Affect a Person's Preferences

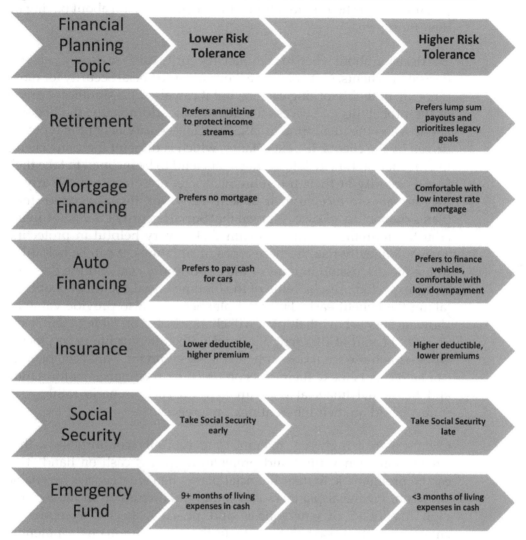

Financial Planning Topic	Lower Risk Tolerance		Higher Risk Tolerance
Retirement	Prefers annuitizing to protect income streams		Prefers lump sum payouts and prioritizes legacy goals
Mortgage Financing	Prefers no mortgage		Comfortable with low interest rate mortgage
Auto Financing	Prefers to pay cash for cars		Prefers to finance vehicles, comfortable with low downpayment
Insurance	Lower deductible, higher premium		Higher deductible, lower premiums
Social Security	Take Social Security early		Take Social Security late
Emergency Fund	9+ months of living expenses in cash		<3 months of living expenses in cash

There are several steps a financial planner can take to reframe financial decisions when clients need help balancing their risk tolerance and their preferences when making financial decisions that will lead to better outcomes. For example, it can be challenging to explain to low risk tolerant clients why their financial plan probability of success drops drastically if they pursue selling half of their investment portfolio to pay off their low interest rate mortgage. In some cases, explaining the of the opportunity cost and lost investment gains and portfolio earning potential can be helpful to reframe the clients' decision about paying off their mortgage.

The decision about when to take Social Security can be a deeply personal decision to clients. Not only have they paid into Social Security for most, if not all, of their working careers, but it can also be a significant driver of the probability of success for their plan. Additionally, the decision about when the ideal time to take a social security benefit is typically driven by the clients' life expectancy, which is difficult for many clients to think about. Low risk tolerant clients tend to be inclined to take their Social Security at their full retirement age, or sometimes as early as they are able to receive their benefit. However, this can reduce their plan's probability of success given that Social Security is a cost-of-living adjusted retirement income stream that is very helpful in protecting against longevity risk. In these types of situations, it can be helpful to frame the discussion in light of the opportunity cost and the decrease in the expected present value of the lifetime Social Security benefits by taking the benefit early. Financial planners can also provide value by showing clients how their plan will change based on taking their Social Security benefit at different ages and with different life expectancies. Discussing these scenarios with their spouse and their financial planner can help clients make their decision based on the financial information and the actual financial risks involved in each scenario rather than purely based on their inherent risk preferences.

Clients with a high risk tolerance are typically comfortable with a smaller emergency fund and prefer to keep less cash on hand. This can be problematic to their financial plan when emergencies inevitable show up. Financial planners can frame the discussion in light of the high likelihood of emergencies and provide specific examples of emergencies. It is also helpful to focus the conversation on the potential consequences of not having sufficient cash on hand (i.e., paying a high interest rate on a HELOC, selling investments when the market is down, paying a tax penalty for pulling money out of retirement accounts, high credit card interest rates, etc.) that are relevant to the client's situation.

1.7 A FRAMEWORK FOR ANALYZING CLIENT FINANCIAL RISK TOLERANCE

Kenneth Ryack, Michael Kraten, and Aamer Sheikh (2016) developed a framework for practitioners to use with their clients to organize different factors on the basis of foreseeability and manageability. Foreseeability means how easily a client can predict a change in a factor. Manageability indicates how much confidence a client expresses they have in their ability to manage the factor's impact on their financial status. The authors suggest that practitioners and their clients jointly work to assign each factor to one of the four categories in Figure 1.5. Based on their risk tolerance, clients may choose to put each factor in different categories. This process should be educational and informative when it comes to learning about your clients' perspectives and what they feel like is uncertain in their lives.

Figure 1.5. Foreseeability and Manageability Factors

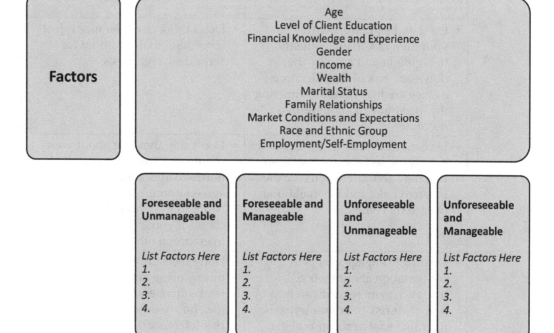

If most personal factors fall into the "foreseeable and manageable"

factors fall into the "unforeseeable and unmanageable" category, the client likely has a lower risk tolerance. If most of the factors fall into the other two categories, further discussion is necessary to understand the implications of the client's risk tolerance and how that may play out in the financial planning process.

1.8 RISK TOLERANCE CONSIDERATIONS: DO'S AND DON'TS

The left-hand side of the chart below contains a list of key things related to financial risk tolerance that are important to do in your work with clients. On the right, the chart contains items that you should avoid doing as they can hurt the connection you are trying to build with your clients. Each of the following chapters contains a do and don't chart that summarizes many of the key points from the chapter.

Do	Don't
• Do spend extra time with your high risk tolerant clients to highlight and amplify the downside risk of their decisions as they are likely underestimating the likelihood of an undesired outcome.	• Don't think risk tolerance is just something to think about for compliance purposes.
• Do carefully consider the best way to frame a decision for clients so that they accurately perceive the inherent risks and the likelihood of each outcome.	• Don't stop thinking about your clients' risk tolerance once their portfolio allocation has been agreed upon. You may experience better follow-through from the clients if you incorporate their risk tolerance in other planning areas.
• Do direcly engage clients in conversation about their risk tolerance to increase awareness of how their risk tolerance impacts their financial decision-making.	• Don't measure risk tolerance purely using heuristics or single-item self assessment questions (i.e., how would you rate your risk tolerance?).

• Do be intentional and creative in incorporating risk-tolerance in your planning materials and discussions with clients. Consider using the risk tolerance framework described in this chapter.	
• Do understand how personal factors such as gender, education, income, and wealth can impact risk tolerance.	

References

Chatterjee, S. and Yeske, D. (2022). Framing advice in light of client's risk tolerance. In S. Chatterjee, S. Lutter and D. Yeske (Eds.), *The Psychology of Financial Planning* (ch. 1). Certified Financial Planner Board of Standards, Inc.

Grable, J. E. (2000). Financial risk tolerance and additional factors that affect risk taking in everyday money matters. *Journal of Business and Psychology, 14*(4), 625-630.

Grable, J. and Lytton, R. H. (1999). Financial risk tolerance revisited: The development of a risk assessment instrument. *Financial Services Review, 8*(3), 163-181.

Jhangiani, R. S., Chiang, I. A., Cuttler, C. and Leighton, D. C. (2019). *Research Methods in Psychology*. Kwantlen Polytechnic University.

Ryack, K. N., Kraten, M. and Sheikh, A. (2016). Incorporating financial risk tolerance research into the financial planning process. *Journal of Financial Planning, 29*(10), 54-61.

Chapter 2

Developing a Productive Client-Planner Relationship that Addresses the Psychological Elements of Financial Planning

2.1 INTRODUCTION

Technology and automation continue to play a larger role both in our everyday lives and in the world of investing. It's possible to have a fully discretionary and well-diversified portfolio managed for costs that are significantly lower than just ten years ago.

So how do firms and practitioners continue to create and maintain a significant value proposition in a world where the investment component has largely become commoditized? For many firms, the transition from full-service investment management to full-service holistic wealth management is a significant strategic priority. Clients can expect to receive greater value from their relationship with their

and services in conjunction with investment management at a similar fee structure.

One thing technology will never be able to replace is the value of the financial-planner relationship. In many helping professions such as therapy and social work, the relationship between the helper and the client is considered to be the most important aspect of determining the outcomes. There are a number of steps financial planners can take to build strong, trusting relationships with their clients.

At the heart of the transition from full-service investment management to full-service holistic wealth management is the topic of financial planning. If executed well, practitioners have the opportunity to "do good by doing good." Although many firms utilize robust financial planning tools and software, the combination of both human and digital capabilities in this regard is critical.

Why is this? Financial well-being is incredibly personal. People work their entire lives to create a financial picture that is the culmination of years of saving and sacrifice. To many, it's not just a number, but rather the result of a journey that was comprised of many emotional high and lows along the way. Each day, people battle with life, death, birth, marriage, divorce, children, college, and the list continues.

To be successful, you must combine the technical skills learned through licensing, training, and certifications in conjunction with the art of behavioral psychology. Financial planning is just as much art as it is science as there are often multiple options and tradeoffs available for clients to consider regarding their financial futures and legacies. Practitioners must learn to first ask comprehensive open-ended questions to paint broad brush strokes as they foster a personal, yet professional, relationship with their clients. Once that broad story can be illustrated, then further honing and clarifying the goals, objectives and potential outcomes becomes a more easily attained reality.

2.2 THE CLIENT-PLANNER RELATIONSHIP IN PRACTICE

[A] The Role of the Practitioner

Done well, an impactful plan will have a positive impact on both the heart and mind. Successful practitioners have the ability to connect, deeply understand, and paint a picture of what's possible regarding a client's financial life. Clients will feel a sense of empowerment, reassurance, hope and direction. They will clearly be able to see the changes that may be needed to achieve those stated goals and aspirations. They will also clearly be able to see the need to change saving or spending habits or risk parameters that are comfortable and acceptable to them.

Most financial plans deliver an output that states whether a plan is "successful" or not using a Monte Carlo simulation where a platform runs multiple iterations of what scenarios might occur in the future. If one's probability of success is high, then the plan is deemed "successful." If the probably of success is low, then the opposite is true. In reality, a plan's "probability of success" is not the end of the planning process, but rather the beginning.

If a practitioner engages with a client on a financial planning consultation, delivers a positive and engaging client experience along with a detailed financial plan, but the client never takes any of the recommended next steps, has the practitioner done their job as a financial professional? You could argue that if the client is not inspired to take action, then the consultation was not successful and actually was wasted time for both the client and practitioner.

More and more frequently, firms are looking to capture the actions that their clients are taking post-planning interaction as this is the true definition of success. Consider John, a practitioner who creates an incredibly robust and detailed plan for his client. He outlines fifteen different recommendations for his client to execute over the course of the next year. His client immediately feels overwhelmed when presented with a to-do list in addition to an already busy life.

[B] Modular Financial Planning

Consider Mary who also engages in a robust planning focus with her client. Although she could identify fifteen individual action steps for her client to take, she only outlines the three most important steps that her client should take immediately. The plan that inspires some action is more impactful than the plan that inspires none. That being said, the practitioner must find a balance between moving the client toward change in a manageable way for the client while also fulfilling their fiduciary duty as a CERTIFIED FINANCIAL PLANNER™. All financial planning areas and recommendations should be addressed during the planning process; however, the practitioner and the client can work together to effectively ensure the recommendations are implemented. Sometimes, this means prioritizing which recommendations to implement first to ensure the client does not become overwhelmed and fails to implement any of the recommendations. In other words, a three-year holistic financial plan broken into manageable pieces may often be a more impactful and realistic approach vs. a one-time plan that could feel overwhelming and overly complex up front.

Finally, it's important for practitioners to be knowledgeable and well-rounded in all wealth management areas that may impact a client's life. Many practitioners have one or two areas of specialty where they are comfortable engaging with clients such as investments or banking. However, it's important for practitioners to know when to leverage all the tools and solutions available to benefit the client. Practitioners should be comfortable discussing all elements of a client's balance sheet to outline a list of recommended steps and/or solutions that would be most beneficial to the client. Subject matter experts can then be utilized if needed to implement individual strategies identified during the planning process.

[C] Financial Planning as a Future Financial Roadmap

Financial planning can be an incredibly personal and emotional experience for many clients. However, one can argue that there is no more important activity when working with clients than to create a future financial roadmap. The benefits to clients can impact family legacies for years to come.

The benefits to practitioners and their firms can be significant also. It's well documented that those clients with a financial plan in place have significantly higher net worth than those without (Finke et al., 2011; Winchester et al., 2011). Clients who engage in powerful and holistic planning experiences are more likely to consolidate assets with that practitioner along with larger utilization of a company's suite of products and services.

Our industry is at an interesting point in its history. What was a value-added service previously is now a base-line expectation. What worked yesterday won't work tomorrow. How can firms and practitioners continue to positively impact the lives of their clients while also ensuring success in their professional careers? At the heart of this wealth management journey is planning. It's critical that practitioners continue to invest in themselves, their knowledge, and their acumen to remain well-positioned for what the future may bring.

[D] Essential Elements for Working with Clients

Now that the importance of the practitioner-client relationship has been established, below are some items from Chapter 2: Developing a Productive Client-Planner Relationship That Addresses the Psychological Elements of Financial Planning in *The Psychology of Financial Planning* (McCoy and Van Zutphen, 2022) that will be helpful as you work to build meaningful relationships with your clients and help them to achieve optimal outcomes.

- Although it may be tempting to just focus on the financial and technical elements of the financial plan, it is important to recognize that our clients' goals and values are much more than just numbers. You must be able to build a rapport and establish trust with your client to develop a strong working relationship.

- Acknowledge that your client has a range of needs. These needs can be visualized based on Maslow's Hierarchy of Needs (see Figure 2.1 below). Understand that personal finances touch each area of your client's intrinsically and extrinsically motivated needs.

Figure 2.1. Maslow's Hierarchy of Needs

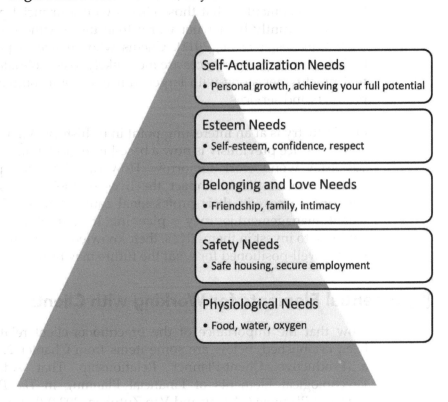

- Money scripts can be thought of as someone's money story. Money scripts are our beliefs about money that have been shaped by our unique experience with money. Understanding your client's money scripts is essential for helping them achieve self-actualization. Money scripts are addressed in more detail in Chapter 5.

- The Transtheoretical Model of Behavior Change is a useful framework that financial planners can use to understand client behavior. Once you've identified which stage of change your client is in, the model can help you identify how you can best move your client closer to taking action and change problematic behaviors.

2.3 TRANSTHEORETICAL MODEL OF BEHAVIOR CHANGE

One of the shortfalls of theory and academic research is typically that it is very difficult to apply in practice or "in the real world." The Transtheoretical

cessation, but it can be applied to any human behavior. It is one of the most useful theories available to financial planners in working with clients. TTM is a tool that can be effectively used to help more clients to implement their plans which is essential given that only about 20% of clients are ready to make changes to their behavior (Prochaska and Velicer, 1997).

The TTM is based on the assumptions that every person is capable of change, behavior change is a cyclical process rather than a linear process or an event, and basic, common principles exist which reveal the structure and process of change regardless of the individual, the behavior, or the circumstances.

The 5 stages in TTM are precontemplation, contemplation, preparation, action, and maintenance (Prochaska et al., 1992). The stage of change indicates where a person is in the process of change.

Figure 2.2. Stages of the Transtheoretical Model of Change Behavior

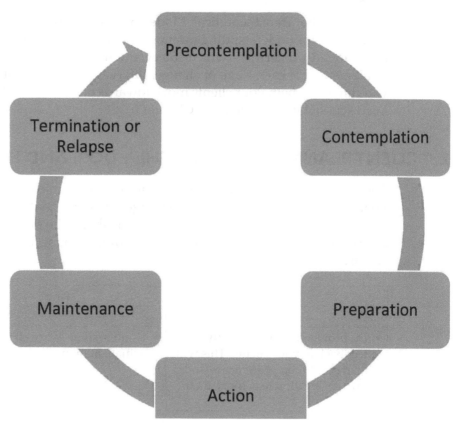

A person in the precontemplation stage fails to admit he or she needs to alter behavior; therefore, he or she has no intention of attempting to achieve change. In order to move to the contemplation stage, the individual must become aware of the need for change even though he or she may not intend to attempt change in the near future. Next, the person will move to the preparation stage where he or she has decided to take specific steps to create change in the near future. In the action stage, the person is actively engaged in the process of behavioral change in order to overcome the problem. In order to make the change permanent, the individual enters the maintenance stage where he or she continues to monitor behavior in order to avoid relapse. Relapse is considered a normal part of the behavior change process. For this reason, we can think of the TTM as a cyclical process. Most people do not move through the stages in a linear manner because many people relapse to their original behavior before they successfully accomplish behavior change.

Although the Transtheoretical Model of Change is useful just as a framework for understanding human behavior, additional research has been done to determine which interventions can be most effectively implemented at each stage of change. Interventions and strategies that you can use to help your clients move towards better financial behavior are discussed in more detail in Chapter 6.

2.4 CLIENT-PLANNER RELATIONSHIP: DO'S AND DON'TS

The left-hand side of the chart below summarizes some of the key steps financial planners can take to build stronger planner-client relationships. The column on the right contains steps that should be avoided as they can be detrimental in your pursuit of building a connection with your clients.

Do	Don't
• Do provide frequent, positive feedback to your clients. This will help build their self-efficacy and their motivation to achieve their goals.	• Don't assume every client's self-actualization needs are the same.

• Do give special attention to your client's self-actualization needs as you develop the financial plan as another way to deepen the planning relationship.	• Don't assume that socialization ends when someone reaches adulthood; it is a lifelong process.
• Do build your client's self-efficacy whenever possible. Increasing their financial literacy is one useful strategy to accomplish this.	• Don't assume your client is ready to change or take action just because they made an appointment to see you.
• Do ask your clients about their childhood experiences with money.	• Don't operate under the assumption that change is easy for your clients.
• Do use the Money Genogram exercise with your clients to help uncover their money story.	• Don't assume that just because your clients relapsed to bad financial behavior that they are incapable of change or will never be able to make the change to better financial behavior.
• Do help your clients build their self-efficacy by creating small tangible tasks that the client can accomplish before the next meeting.	
• Do help your clients build their self-efficacy by helping them discover their preferred learning style. Adapt your engagement with them to account for their preferred learning style.	
• Do frame a relapse as a hiccup in their financial journey that can easily be overcome.	
• Do be genuinely curious.	

References

Finke, M. S., Huston, S. J. and Winchester, D. D. (2011). Financial advice: Who pays. *Journal of Financial Counseling and Planning*, 22(1), 18-26.

McCoy, M. and Van Zutphen, N. (2022). Developing a productive client-planner relationship that addresses the psychological elements of financial planning. In S. Chatterjee, S. Lutter and D. Yeske (Eds.), *The Psychology of Financial Planning* (ch. 2). Certified Financial Planner Board of Standards, Inc.

Prochaska, J. O., DiClemente, C. C., and Norcross, J. C. (1992). In search of how people change: Applications to addictive behaviors. *American Psychologist, 47*, 1102-1114.

Prochaska J.O. and Velicer, W.F. (1997). The transtheoretical model of health behavior change. *American Journal of Health Promotion, 12*(1), 38-48.

Winchester, D. D., Huston, S. J. and Finke, M. S. (2011). Investor prudence and the role of financial advice. *Journal of Financial Service Professionals, 65*(4), 43-51.

Chapter 3

Identifying and Responding to Client Values and Goals

3.1 INTRODUCTION

Goals are foundational to a client's financial plan. When building a financial plan, typically a financial planner will go through a discovery process to determine the client's current financial information as well as establishing a relationship with the client. The financial plan is a roadmap demonstrating to your clients how they will move from their current situation to accomplishing their goals. As part of the Practice Standards for the Financial Planning Process, CFP Board mandates that data be gathered about qualitative factors such as the client's values, attitudes, expectations, goals, and priorities (CFP Board, n.d.).

> **Personal Values**
>
> A personal value is desirable state, objective, goal, or behavior that people use to judge and choose between what is "good" or "bad" for themselves and for society. Values are chosen to support the person's well-being though over the well-being of society. In other words, values are very personal.

The focus of this chapter is to provide resources for practitioners as they gather data about clients' goals and values as well as how they should communicate with clients about their goals and values. A personal value is a desirable state, objective, goal, or behavior that people use to judge and choose between what is "good" or "bad" for themselves and for society (Sagie and Elizur, 1996). Values are chosen to support the person's well-being though over the well-being of society. In other words, values are very personal. On the other hand, a goal can be thought of as a specific aim or purpose (Cambridge Dictionary, n.d.). Typically, when someone has a goal, they have set themselves some objective that they would like to accomplish. Although goals may change over time, values tend to be much more stable and don't tend to change much over time.

> **Goals**
>
> A goal can be thought of as a specific aim or purpose. Typically, when someone has a goal, they have set themselves some objective that they would like to accomplish.

3.2 IDENTIFYING CLIENT'S GOALS IN PRACTICE

In practice, it takes time and intentional investment in the client relationship to understand the client's values. Typically, it is much easier for clients to identify their goals than it is for them to identify their underlying values. As an additional complicating factor, partners within a household likely have some different values and goals. During a financial planning engagement the process of discussing goals is typically more overt than the process of discussing values. Some financial planners may feel uncomfortable asking their clients directly to describe their values. Financial planners skeptical of gathering data about client values may be surprised by the richness and the depth of discussion these types of questions can create. Clients may also feel more motivated to take action to implement the recommendations once they can directly tie their goals in the financial plan to their personal values.

There are a number of ways practitioners can go about gathering data about client's goals and values. This may take the form of questionnaires or assessments administered during the intake process. Other planners may prefer to structure the data gathering process more informally, asking questions about goals and values during a meeting. Yet others

Below are a few key pieces of information from Chapter 3: Identifying and Responding to Client Values and Goals in *The Psychology of Financial Planning* (McCoy and Lurtz, 2022) that will be helpful to a practitioner.

- It is probably impossible to understand every facet of your clients' identities.

- Clients' values shape their goals. Clients' values are shaped by their culture. Culture includes race, gender, identity, ability, age, ethnicity, and religion.

- It can be very detrimental to the client-planner relationship to rely on stereotypes. It is much more effective to approach each new client relationship and planning engagement with an open mind and genuine curiosity.

- It is common for financial planners and clients to disagree on how money should be used for goals. Strong communication skills and certain techniques (e.g., nonviolent communication) may be particularly helpful in resolving the conflict or finding alignment between planner and client.

- It is essential for you to understand your own values and identity before trying to understand your clients' values and identity. Your values and identity shape the recommendations you provide and how you communicate with clients, so it is important for you to understand how this may create a bias or influence your conclusions.

3.3 IDENTIFYING YOUR OWN VALUES

As you start having conversations with your clients about their values and what is important in their lives, you should go through a similar exercise with yourself. It is important to respect your clients' values even though they may be different from your own. It is also important to understand how your own values impact your decisions so that you can help guide your clients through a similar process.

There are a number of different values assessments you can purchase online. However, there are also some exercises you can do that may help

(https://brenebrown.com/resources/living-into-our-values/) that will guide you through an exercise to help you identify your values. She also has a podcast episode (including a transcript of the podcast episode) guiding you through the worksheet (Brown and Guillen, 2022).

Other useful exercises that you may wish to use personally or with your clients include building a life wheel or building a journey map (Nash, 2022).

3.4 IDENTIFYING AND ADDRESSING CLIENT'S CULTURAL VALUES

One way to differentiate between different cultures is to understand that some cultures tend to be more collectivistic while other cultures are more individualistic. Figure 3.1 below summarizes how people from collectivistic cultures may prioritize certain financial aspects or may have different goals than someone from an individualistic culture. This chart is intended to portray cultural tendencies, so don't assume that these characteristics will hold true for every person. However, it may be useful as you formulate your questions to understand your client's goals from a cultural standpoint.

Figure 3.1. Prioritization of Financial Aspects in Collectivistic and Individualistic Cultures

3.5 HOW TO USE NONVIOLENT COMMUNICATION TO RESPOND TO CLIENTS

There are two main sets of communication strategies that advisors can use to overcome goal incongruence between the advisor and the client(s). Therapeutic communication strategies are covered in more detail in Chapter 13. Nonviolent communication (NVC), however, is described in this section because it is particularly helpful when there are conflicting goals and values occurring in a planner-client interaction. The four steps to nonviolent communication are described in more detail in Figure 3.2 below.

Figure 3.2. Four Steps to Nonviolent Communication

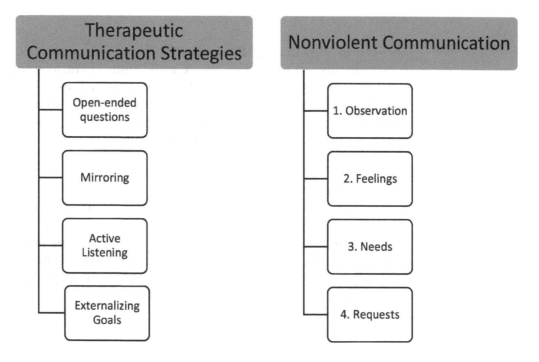

1. *Observation*

    Observation is the first step of nonviolent communication. You should state what the problem is to your client. Be careful to do this without bias or casting blame. Be sure you are using a neutral tone. Focus on what you observe in the current moment

2. *Feelings*

The second step calls you to share your feelings. Be careful to distinguish feelings from general thoughts. This technique does not call upon you to share your general thoughts in this moment. Rather, focus on your emotional and physiological sensations only.

3. *Needs*

In the third step, you must articulate what needs that you have that are not being met. You can lay out how your goals and the client's goals are incongruent.

4. *Requests*

The fourth step creates the opportunity for some action or transformation to occur and for you and your client to come closer to some resolution. You should lay out your request clearly and succinctly. Be as specific as you can. It is important to make the request while you are in the midst of this conversation. Resist the urge to wait until later or send your request in a follow-up email.

The Center for Nonviolent Communication has put together a free Nonviolent Communication Instruction Self-Guide (The Center for Nonviolent Communication, n.d.) which lays out an abundance of resources to help you learn about nonviolent communication. You can think of the basic model of nonviolent communication as it is laid out in Figure 3.3 and on the Center for Nonviolent Communication's website.

Figure 3.3. Model of Nonviolent Communication

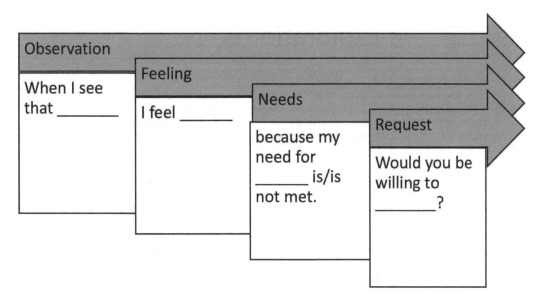

3.6 ADDITIONAL RESOURCES FOR FINANCIAL PLANNING PRACTITIONERS

Roy Diliberto (2006) published several worksheets in the Journal of Financial Planning which are adapted from his book, *Financial Planning-The Next Step: Merging Your Client's Money with Their Lives*. The article lays out how the worksheets should be used as well as listing 21 questions that planners should use to uncover more information about client's values and personal histories.

George Kinder and colleagues (2005) developed the EVOKE methodology for obtaining a better understanding of your clients' goals. Figure 3.4 provides more details about each of the 5 parts of the EVOKE process.

Figure 3.4. The EVOKE Process

E   Exploration

- Use open-ended questions
- Ask: "Why are you here?"
- Ask: "What would you like to see happen in this meeting or the series of meetings we might have together?"
- Listen actively and carefully to the client's responses. Use reflective listening techniques.
- Do not take control of the conversation or share your own views until closer to the end of the conversation.
- Use a phrase like "Is that all?" to encourage the client to think through their responses and share additional information.

V   Vision

- Make sure you have gathered the client's relevant financial information before the meeting.
- Ask: "I want you to imagine that you are financially secure, that you have enough money to take care of your needs, now and in the future. How would you live your life? What would you do with the money? Would you change anything? Let yourself go. Don't hold back your dreams. Describe a life that is complete, that is richly yours."
- Ask: "This time you visit your doctor who tells you that you have five to ten years left to live. The good part is that you won't ever feel sick. The bad news is that you will have no notice of the moment of your death. What will you do in the time you have remaining to live? Will you change your life? How will you do it?"
- Ask: "This time your doctor shocks you with the news that you have only one day left to live. Notice what feelings arise as you confront your very real mortality. Ask yourself: What dreams will be left unfullfilled. What do I wish I had finished or had been? What do I wish I had done? What did I miss?"
- Be open while the client answers. Do not prejudge. Be empathetic. Bring inspiration to the conversation.

O   Obstacles

- Outline the obstacles to accomplishing the vision together with the client.
- Consider obvious obstacles and obstacles that may be harder to identify.
- Encourage the client to come up with solutions or strategies to overcome the obstacles. Brainstorm and use creative thinking together.
- Challenge defeatist attitudes, constricted thinking, or unrealistic timelines.
- Applaud and encourage effective solutions to the obstacles.

K   Knowledge

- Take the lead in the conversation and bring your expertise and technical knowledge into the conversation and the development of the plan.
- When you present the plan, acknowledge and empower the client's vision. This will instill confidence in the client.

E   Execution

- Coach the client through implementing the recommendations. Follow-up with the clinet, encourage the client, and applaud the client as implementation proceeds.
- Monitor and update the plan periodically

3.7 GOALS AND VALUES: DO'S AND DON'TS

The left-hand side of the chart below summarizes some of the key steps financial planners can take to identify clients' goals and values. The column on the right contains steps that should be avoided as they can be detrimental in your pursuit of building a connection with your clients.

Do	Don't
• Do seek out resources to develop a systematic practice for discovering and addressing client values.	• Don't stereotype.
• Do collect both quantitative AND qualitative data about your clients goals and values during the data gathering process.	• Don't be afraid to ask client's "why?" Understanding their "why" can provide you with insight into their financial decision-making process and the values that drive their financial behavior.
• Do check in with your clients periodically to determine whether their goals have changed.	• Don't avoid difficult conversations. Use the skills discussed in this chapter to approach these difficult discussions. You may develop a deeper relationship with your client, develop deeper trust, or learn something new about your client.
• Do understand how beliefs, values, and goals directly impact financial behavior in terms of earning, spending, and saving.	• Don't be afraid to practice communication techniques before you use them with clients. Find a coworker or a friend to talk through how you might approach some difficult situations.
• Do slow down and provide structure when facing a difficult conversation	• Don't skip Chapter 15. Empathy and honesty are essential parts of effective nonviolent communication.
• Do understand that the inherent trust a client has in you can be	

• Do use a variety of communication strategies to gather data about your clients' values and goals.	
• Do use new communication techniques in lower stakes conversations before trying a new technique (i.e., nonviolent communication) in a high stakes situation to develop your comfort level and skill.	
• Do acknowledge when clients are being vulnerable with you and thank them for trusting you and/or trying new communication techniques with you.	
• Do seek out additional training. Money Quotient, The Kinder Institute, and Advisor Roadmap have helpful resources and training programs that may be helpful as you work to discovering and dicussing client goals and values in a culturally sensitive way.	

References

Brown, B. (n.d.). *Living into out values.* Brené Brown. https://brenebrown.com/resources/living-into-our-values/.

Brown, B. and Guillen, B. (Hosts). (2022, January 26). Living into our values (No. 89) [Audio podcast episode]. In *Unlocking us with Brené Brown.* https://brenebrown.com/podcast/living-into-our-values/.

Cambridge Dictionary. (n.d.). Goal. In *Cambridge Dictionary.com.* https://dictionary.cambridge.org/us/dictionary/english/goal.

CFP Board. (n.d.). *Code of Ethics and Standards of Conduct.* https://www.cfp.net/ethics/code-of-ethics-and-standards-of-conduct.

Diliberto, R. (2006). Uncovering and understanding your clients' history, values, and transitions. *Journal of Financial Planning, 19*(12), 52-59.

Kinder, G. and Galvan, S. (2005). EVOKE™: A life planning methodology for the coming revolution in client relationships. *Journal of Financial Planning, 18*(4), 46-55.

McCoy, M. and Lurtz, M. (2022). Identifying and responding to client values and goals. In S. Chatterjee, S. Lutter and D. Yeske (Eds.), *The Psychology of Financial Planning* (ch. 3).

Nash, J. (2020 November 26). What are your personal values? *Harvard Business Review.* https://hbr.org/2020/11/what-are-your-personal-values.

Sagie, A. and Elizur, D. (1996). The structure of personal values: A conical representation of multiple life areas. *Journal of Organizational Behavior, 17*(S1), 573-586.

The Center for Nonviolent Communication. (n.d.). *NVC instruction self-guide.* CNVC.org. https://www.cnvc.org/online-learning/nvc-instruction-guide/nvc-instruction-guide.

Chapter 4

Impact of Cognitive Biases and Heuristics on Financial Decision-making and Well-being

4.1 INTRODUCTION

It is essential for financial planners to understand how cognitive biases and heuristics impact not only their clients, but also themselves. Although much of economic theory assumes that people always make completely rational decisions, it is well documented that our brains can make errors in predictable and systematic ways. Scientists and researchers have been studying our brains and how we make all kinds of decisions, including financial decisions. As a result of this research, a number of cognitive biases and heuristics have been identified and studied within the context of behavioral finance. Cognitive biases occur when individuals make an error in their decision-making process (Sages and Chatterjee, 2022). Heuristics are mental shortcuts that people use

> **Cognitive Biases**
>
> Cognitive biases occur when individuals make an error in their decision-making process.

choices and judgements needed to find a solution to the problem (Sages and Chatterjee, 2022). Both heuristics and cognitive biases are always at play in the financial planning process. Understanding when your clients may be susceptible to them, and even when you yourself as a planner are susceptible to them, will make you a better financial planner.

> **Heuristics**
>
> Heuristics are mental short-cuts that people use to make the decision-making process easier. Heuristics simplify the choices and judgement needed to find a solution to the problem.

The behavioral biases and heuristics laid out in this chapter are not necessarily a "good" or a "bad" thing. They describe and help us to understand how our brains work. Some would argue that cognitive biases and heuristics can even make us better decision-makers under certain conditions (Tharp, 2019).

4.2 COGNITIVE BIASES AND HEURISTICS IN PRACTICE

The bulleted list below underscores some of the most applicable concepts for practitioners from Chapter 4: Impact of Cognitive Biases and Heuristics on Financial Decision-making and Well-being in *The Psychology of Financial Planning* (Sages and Chatterjee, 2022).

- Biases and heuristics are present at every stage in the financial planning process. They can often lead to clients being resistant to financial planner's advice or failing to implement recommendations.

- Once you can recognize and identifying biases and heuristics, you will be able to work with your clients to be able to overcome them, hopefully leading to better financial decisions and outcomes for you and your clients.

- Decision-making can be categorized into two systems of thinking. System 1 decisions are made intuitively but are typically very susceptible to cognitive biases and heuristics. System 2 decisions utilize reflective thinking and requires slower, more deliberate, logical thinking. System 2 thinking results in better decisions but requires more time energy than

System 1 thinking. Create a system and environment at work where more System 2 thinking can occur.

- Financial planners can reduce the bias that can occur during decision-making by modifying their own decision-making processes and altering their environment. Specific strategies for doing so are discussed later in the chapter.

4.3 CLIENT COGNITIVE BIASES AND HEURISTICS

Each of the cognitive biases and heuristics discussed in this chapter are introduced and defined in Chapter 4: Impact of Cognitive Biases and Heuristics on Financial Decision-making and Well-being in *The Psychology of Financial Planning* (Sages and Chatterjee, 2022). This section will focus on how to help your clients who are making detrimental decisions due to cognitive biases and heuristics. This may also be helpful in your own decision-making as well.

[A] Availability Bias

How to recognize it: You make decisions based on the first thing that comes to your mind, and you discount other relevant information. You may be overvaluing information that you gained from repeated, emotional, or personal experiences.

How to address it: Try to avoid making decisions too quickly or based on just one or two factors that first come to mind ("Availability Heuristic," n.d.).

[B] Salience Bias

How to recognize it: You or your client overvalue information that feels more vivid or makes you feel some emotion when you are making a decision.

How to address it: Avoid making a snap decision based on a "gut" feeling. Provide feedback to your clients in the moment and draw attention to how they are using information in their decision-making ("Salience Bias," n.d.).

[C] Recency Bias

How to recognize it: You or your client tends to focus on recent events and recently learned information. Recently learned information seems more important or more reliable than information received previously.

How to address it: Intentionally work to increase what you consider to be the "recent" past, both with yourself and your client (Richards, n.d.). Be intentional about considering the bigger picture.

[D] Persuasion Bias

How to recognize it: You or your client make decisions based on information that you have heard frequently, regardless of whether or not the information is correct. You are more likely to assume information you have heard multiple times is correct without doing your own research.

How to address it: Ensure information is accurate before making a decision. Do your best to be aware of persuasion bias when making decisions and be sure to objectively weigh all options before making recommendations.

[E] Familiarity Bias

How to recognize it: You or your client give greater weight to information that you or your client has personal familiarity with. Client who prefer to hold a larger than recommended amount of stock in the company they works for or clients who show a preference for domestic equities over domestic equities may be experiencing familiarity bias.

How to address it: Explain the importance of a diversified portfolio to your clients. Ensure you are researching a wide variety of asset classes or develop a systematic way to evaluate investments for consideration in your model portfolios.

[F] Anchoring

How to recognize it: If clients seem fixated on a specific statistic, fact, or figure and use it as a foundation for a decision, they may be experiencing

How to address it: Research decisions thoroughly. If you've identified a client's anchor, it can be helpful to bring the reference point to their attention or even try to move the reference point, if appropriate. Firstly, it is important to acknowledge anchoring bias. Delaying or slowing down the decision-making process can be helpful. Additionally, you should ensure your own reference points in decision-making are accurate and relevant or try to remove your anchor to the reference point completely (Krockow, 2019).

[G] Mental Accounting

How to recognize it: Clients treat money in different accounts or money from different sources differently.

How to address it: Help your clients create a cash flow statement or a budget or spending plan. Discuss how any unexpected windfalls will be allocated ("Mental Accounting," n.d.). If you identify mental accounting occurring, describe the bias that mental accounting creates and how a dollar is always worth a dollar, regardless of its source, so dollars from different sources should be treated the same way.

[H] Representativeness Bias

How to recognize it: You or your client believe that past returns are indicative of future returns. Another way that representativeness bias can be displayed is through an overreliance on stereotypes when making decisions.

How to address it: Representativeness bias is a particularly difficult bias to avoid or correct. Awareness can be helpful in avoiding the bias. Otherwise, formal training in logical thinking or a nudge to "think like a statistician" may be helpful ("Representativeness Heuristic," n.d.).

[I] Law of Small Numbers

How to recognize it: You or your client place an overemphasis on the significance of trends from a small amount of data. You believe that if a trend starts to develop, that trend is more likely to continue than it actually is. You may also believe that a stock's performance over a relatively short period of time (i.e., a week, a month) is representative

How to address it: It can be helpful to challenge the assumptions that lead to a particular conclusion (i.e., why do you think stock ABC is going to continue its current trajectory?) (Shatz, n.d.). Other techniques described previously may also be helpful such as taking more time to make decisions and educating yourself about these biases to increase awareness.

[J] Gambler's Fallacy

How to recognize it: You or your client believe that true probabilities will be exhibited or displayed over the course of a limited number of occurrences. For example, you or your client may believe that a certain event may be more or less likely to occur because it happened in the past. In reality, whether that event occurred previously or not does not impact the future probability of the event occurring again or not. For example, the fact that your dog developed an expensive chronic condition does not affect the probability that your cat will also develop an expensive chronic condition. These two events are independent of each other, even though it may initially feel unlikely that both of your pets will be expensive money pits, it is certainly possible.

How to address it: Gambler's fallacy can be particularly difficult to address outside of the gambling context because it can be difficult to understand the true probabilities of events that may happen in normal life. It can be helpful to recognize causal independence of events and thinking through the process by which events truly occur and unfold ("Gambler's Fallacy," n.d.).

[K] Status Quo Bias

How to recognize it: Your clients consistently fails to take action. They consistently counter your recommendations by explaining what they currently are doing is better.

How to address it: Avoid confronting the client. Use listening techniques (see chapter 13) and encourage your clients to restate their motivation for making changes in their financial lives (Lawson and Klontz, 2017).

[L] Sunk Cost Fallacy

How to recognize it: You or your client fail to see that nothing in the past can be changed and that the past should not impact future decisions. For example, your clients may not want to sell an investment that currently has a loss and want to wait until they break even at least. They fail to see that the stock price may never recover to the price they purchased at and that they will still come out ahead by reinvesting the proceeds into a better investment.

How to address it: Learn to recognize when a sunk cost is being involved in decision-making in both your own decisions and your clients. Once a sunk cost has been identified, it becomes easier to exclude from a decision ("Sunk Cost Fallacy," n.d.).

[M] Flat Rate Bias

How to recognize it: Your client wants to buy an annuity, even though you have advised them that the annuity is very expensive and would result in lower sustainable portfolio distributions throughout retirement.

How to address it: Focus on the big picture with your client. Emphasize that the financial plan is built around helping them maximize their goals (and potentially maximizing their net worth). Build a well-diversified, optimized portfolio (Fidelity Viewpoints, 2022).

[N] Endowment Effect

How to recognize it: Your clients are loath to make changes to their investment portfolio. This may occur when they first become a client and are reluctant for you to sell their current holdings or it could be exhibited through reluctance to implement other types of recommendations throughout the planning process. The endowment effect could be at play if clients do not want to surrender an annuity or a life insurance policy because they are overvaluing the assets they personally own.

How to address it: There are three main strategies to counteract the endowment effect. Firstly, it is important to avoid psychological ownership, feeling a sense of mental or emotional ownership of an asset or product. Secondly, always consider opportunity costs when deciding to keep or sell an asset or investment. Finally, always consider market prices when making decisions to buy or sell ("Endowment Effect," n.d.).

[O] Confirmation Bias

How to recognize it: You or your client seek out information that supports your preexisting opinions. Confirmation bias may also lead to a tendency to reject or discount information that contradicts preexisting opinions or beliefs. For example, if you are skeptical of a particular investment or tax strategy and you are only looking for information that confirms your beliefs about this investment or strategy, you are exhibiting confirmation bias.

How to address it: Research opportunities and strategies in a neutral and unbiased manner. Educate your clients about the information they are missing when you recognize they are exhibiting confirmation bias. Seek out differing opinions and be open to alternative views or dissenting opinions.

[P] Cognitive Dissonance

How to recognize it: You or your clients justify your actions and/or change your viewpoint when your behavior conflicts with long-held attitudes or beliefs. You or your client feel or describe feeling internal or mental conflict after making a decision or behaving a certain way. For example, your frugal client decides to spend several months of income on an unnecessary purchase such as an expensive piece of artwork or a collectible. Afterwards, they try to justify the purchase as an investment in an appreciating asset due to the mental conflict created by spending the money on the collectible instead of putting the money aside for their large down payment savings goal.

How to address it: Since cognitive dissonance typically occurs after a decision has been made or an action has been taken, typically little can be done to remove the source of the cognitive dissonance. You and your clients will need to find different ways to address the internal conflict. Being mindful of cognitive inconsistencies can be helpful. Sometimes it may be appropriate to challenge your current beliefs or justify your current behavior. You must decide whether your preexisting beliefs align more closely with your beliefs or whether the behavior you exhibited aligns more closely with your beliefs going forward (Neuhaus, 2021).

4.4 BEHAVIORAL COACHING

Although the biases and heuristics described in the research have been documented thoroughly, there is little academic research available to help clients and financial planners to address and rectify their flawed and biased thinking and decision-making.

As you've read earlier in this chapter, one of the first pieces of advice to improve decision-making is typically to provide education about behavioral finance biases or to increase awareness of flawed decision-making. This is not always the best approach or effective enough to resolve problematic thinking. Financial planning practitioners that have developed an expertise in behavioral finance issues typically recommend behavioral coaching as one option to address these issues.

Behavioral coaching can be used to teach, train, and guide a client to learning a new behavior or change their current behavior (Sam, 2013). Financial planners may be able to facilitate behavior change by prompting or guiding a client's thinking to create an environment where behavior change can happen.

Jay Mooreland (2020), founder of The Behavioral Finance Network, says that behavioral coaching still has an educational component, but the education must be delivered in a specific way. Educating a client with factual statements or providing them with a white paper will not produce the desired results. He recommends "consistently and proactively teaching correct perceptions and reinforcing realistic expectations using timely examples." In his blog post on the Kitces.com Nerd's Eye View blog, he lays out some practical ideas for creating well timed behavioral finance content that your clients will actually read.

4.5 COGNITIVE BIASES AND HEURISTICS: DO'S AND DON'TS

The left-hand side of the chart below summarizes some of the key steps financial planners can take to identify cognitive biases and heuristics. The column on the right contains steps that should be avoided as they can be detrimental in your pursuit of building a connection with your clients.

Do	Don't
• Do educate yourself about behavioral biases and heuristics, and learn to recognize how you and your clients display them.	• Don't assume understanding and learning about behavioral biases will make you immune to these biases.
• Do practice situational awareness whenever possible.	• Don't assume education about biases alone will help your clients change behavior or correct their thinking.
• Do understand the four factors that can lead to more biased decision-making: distraction, fatigue, individual differences, and visceral influences (see Chapter 4 in *The Psychology of Financial Planning*).	• Don't exhibit the herding bias or herding behavior when making financial recommendations (see Chapter 4 in *The Psychology of Financial Planning*).
• Do use checklists as a planning tool with clients to help them de-bias their thinking.	
• Do use "nudges" (see Chapter 5) to modify the decision-making environment.	

References

Fidelity Viewpoints. (2022, April 5). 6 biggest pitfalls for advisors. *Fidelity*. https://www.fidelity.com/viewpoints/personal-finance/financial-improvement.

Krockow, E. M. (2019, February 11). Outsmarting the anchoring bias in three simple steps: Psychological insights can help you avoid the trap of cognitive biases. *Psychology Today*. https://www.psychologytoday.com/us/blog/stretching-theory/201902/outsmart-the-anchoring-bias-in-three-simple-steps.

Lawson, D. R. and Klontz, B. T. (2017). Integrating behavioral finance, financial psychology, and financial therapy theory and techniques into the financial planning process. *Journal of Financial Planning, 30*(7), 48-55.

Mooreland, J. (2020, May 13). Using behavioral finance principles to behaviorally coach clients to make better decisions. *Kitces.com*. https://www.kitces.com/blog/behavioral-finance-network-jay-mooreland-behavior-coaching-financial-decison-making/.

Neuhaus, M. (2021, February 8). Cognitive dissonance: Theory, examples & how to reduce it. *PositivePsychology.com*. https://positivepsychology.com/cognitive-dissonance-theory/.

Richards, C. (n.d.). *The problem with recency bias, and how to fix it*. BehaviorGap.com. https://behaviorgap.com/the-problem-with-recency-bias-and-how-to-fix-it/.

Sages, R. and Chatterjee, S. (2022). Impact of cognitive biases and heuristics on financial decision-making and well-being. In S. Chatterjee, S. Lutter and D. Yeske (Eds.), *The Psychology of Financial Planning* (pp. 57-73). Certified Financial Planner Board of Standards, Inc.

Sam, N. (2013). Behavioral coaching. In *PsychologyDictionary.org*. https://psychologydictionary.org/behavioral-coaching/.

Shatz, I. (n.d.). The law of small numbers: Overestimating the representativeness of small samples. *Effectiviology*. https://effectiviology.com/law-of-small-numbers/#How_to_reduce_your_own_belief_in_the_law_of_small_numbers.

Tharp, D. (2019, September 18). When heuristics and biases may actually improve decision-making. *Kitces.com*. https://www.kitces.com/blog/behavioral-finance-heuristics-bias-positive-outcomes-improve-financial-decision-making/.

Why are we likely to continue with an investment even if it would be rational to give it up? The sunk cost fallacy, explained. (n.d.). The Decision Lab. https://thedecisionlab.com/biases/the-sunk-cost-fallacy.

Why do we focus on items or information that are more prominent and ignore those that are not? The salience bias, explained. (n.d.). The Decision Lab. https://thedecisionlab.com/biases/salience-bias.

Why do we tend to think that things that happened recently are more likely to happen again? The availability heuristic, explained. (n.d.). The Decision Lab. https://thedecisionlab.com/biases/availability-heuristic.

Why do we think a random event is more or less likely to occur if it happened several times in the past? Gambler's fallacy, explained. (n.d.). The Decision Lab. https://thedecisionlab.com/biases/gamblers-fallacy.

Why do we think less about some purchases than others? Mental accounting, explained. (n.d.). The Decision Lab. https://thedecisionlab.com/biases/mental-accounting.

Why do we use similarity to gauge statistical probability? The representativeness heuristic, explained. (n.d.). The Decision Lab. https://thedecisionlab.com/biases/representativeness-heuristic.

Why do we value items more if they belong to us? The endowment effect, explained. (n.d.). The Decision Lab. https://thedecisionlab.com/biases/endowment-effect.

Chapter 5

Client Psychology Barriers in the Financial Planning Process and Strategies for Overcoming Them

5.1 INTRODUCTION

Client psychology impacts the client's objectives, goals, understanding, decision-making, and actions. As such, it is imperative for financial planners to understand how to address the client's psychology barriers, particularly when these barriers are impacting the client's financial plan or even impacting the client personally.

Clients' psychology includes their financial comfort zone, their financial socialization, their money beliefs, and their past financial experiences and behaviors. No two clients will have the same client psychology factors because no two people have the same lived experience. As such, financial planners should endeavor to

Financial Comfort Zone

A state of perceived well-being resulting from familiarity with a set of financial matters or financial experiences that people encounter on a frequent basis.

factors to gain a better understanding of the client's financial behaviors as well as how to overcome any barriers to action that may be present.

A client's financial comfort zone is "a state of perceived well-being resulting from familiarity with a set of financial matters or financial experiences that people encounter on a frequent basis" (Sages and Chatterjee, 2022). Financial planners should endeavor to help their clients remain in their financial comfort zone and ensure the clients' perceptions of good financial well-being matches reality. If clients are outside their financial comfort zone, they are likely to feel unhappy with their financial situation.

> **Money Beliefs**
>
> Preconceived notions or patterns of beliefs that people hold about their money and their finances.

> **Financial Socialization**
>
> The development of one's financial values, attitudes and behaviors that inculcate a sense of financial responsibility and subsequently facilitate financial well-being in later life.

Financial socialization also plays a role in client psychology. Financial socialization means "the development of one's financial values, attitudes and behaviors that inculcate a sense of financial responsibility and subsequently facilitate financial well-being in later life" (Sages and Chatterjee, 2022). Financial socialization usually starts at an early age by learning financial values, attitudes and behaviors from parents or other influential people. Some of this learning is conscious (i.e., being shown how to open a bank account by a parent), but some of the learning also occurs subconsciously (i.e., a person learning to feel that carrying tens of thousands of credit card debt is normal due to parents carrying a large credit card debt load). Financial planners can learn a lot about the reasons for their client's financial attitudes and behaviors by understanding how they were socialized financially. It is worthwhile for financial planners to consider their own financial socialization and how their money behaviors and money beliefs have been shaped by socialization.

Brad Klontz, developer of the Klontz Money Script Inventory, defines money scripts as patterns of beliefs that people hold about their money and their finances (Klontz et al., 2011). It is possible to hold hundreds of different money scripts, and each person's set of money scripts will be different. These money scripts play a large role in shaping the client's actions and decisions.

5.2 CLIENT PSYCHOLOGY BARRIERS IN PRACTICE

Chapter 4 described many of the cognitive biases and errors in thinking that systematically impact decision-making and financial behavior. The client psychology factors described above (financial comfort zone, financial socialization, and money beliefs) also impact clients' decision-making and behavior. Although these factors impact the client at each step in the financial planning process, most practitioners do not gather information about client psychological factors during the data gathering process.

The list below contains helpful information from Chapter 5: Client Psychology Barriers in the Financial Planning Process and Strategies for Overcoming Them in *The Psychology of Financial Planning* (Sages and Chatterjee, 2022).

- Clients make many decisions subconsciously, and typically they make decisions to bring them closer to their equilibrium financial comfort zone.

- Clients learn many of their financial attitudes and money scripts from their parents. This can contribute to both positive and negative outcomes for the client depending on the attitudes and beliefs they learned. It may be worth exploring with clients how problematic money scripts and attitudes developed over time to see whether adjustments can be made.

- Times of transition can create behavioral concerns and potential conflicts between clients and members of the family. This may be particularly relevant for financial planners that are assisting their clients with business transition plans. The Fredo Effect describes the situation where a disappointed family undermines the business transition either consciously or unconsciously.

- Stress and intense emotions can override thinking in the neocortex, the part of the brain responsible for higher cognitive functions and the ability to regulate instinctual responses.

5.3 PATHOLOGICAL FINANCIAL BEHAVIORS

Some clients may display pathological financial behaviors. These behaviors are typically destructive behaviors that are engaged in obsessively or compulsively. Sometimes it can be difficult to determine whether a financial behavior reaches the pathological level.

The sections below are is designed to help you identify whether one of your clients may be experiencing any of these pathological financial behaviors. Questionnaires from the Klontz Money Behavior Inventory are presented to provide additional context for signs that a client's behavior may have reached a pathological level (Klontz et al., 2012). You may not wish or may not be able to ask the clients the questions directly, but you can listen for the statements from the scales in your conversations with clients. You could also use the scale questions as a guide as you structure probing questions. For example, if you believe your client may have Compulsive Buying Disorder, you could ask them, "do you feel in control of your spending?" or "do you feel guilt or shame after going shopping?" Lastly, each section provides some information about the next steps you can take to help your clients with pathological financial behaviors.

[A] Compulsive Buying Disorder

How to recognize it: Compulsive Buying Disorder (CBD) is characterized by obsessive shopping and purchasing behavior which leads to distress or financial hardship (Black, 2007). CBD is estimated to impact just under 6% of the US population. Clients with impulse control disorders such mood, anxiety, substance abuse, or eating disorders are more likely to have CBD. CBD also tends to run in families. If the client is experiencing feelings of guilt or shame due to compulsive shopping or if shopping is impacting the client's relationships, it is possible the client is experiencing CBD.

How to measure it:

Compulsive Buying	Strongly Disagree	Disagree	Disagree A Little	Agree A Little	Agree	Strongly Agree
My spending feels out of control.	1	2	3	4	5	6
I obsess about shopping.	1	2	3	4	5	6
I buy more things than I need or can afford.	1	2	3	4	5	6
I feel irresistible urges to shop.	1	2	3	4	5	6
I shop to forget about my problems and make myself feel better.	1	2	3	4	5	6
I feel guilt and/or shame after making purchases.	1	2	3	4	5	6
I often return items because I feel bad about buying them.	1	2	3	4	5	6
I have tried to reduce my spending but have had trouble doing so.	1	2	3	4	5	6
I hide my spending from my partner/family.	1	2	3	4	5	6
I feel anxious or panicky if I am unable to shop.	1	2	3	4	5	6
Shopping interferes with my work or relationships.	1	2	3	4	5	6

How to address it: CBD is difficult to treat, and it well beyond the scope of a typical financial planner to treat CBD. Financial planners should refer their clients with suspected CBD to a qualified mental health professional, ideally someone with extensive experience working with CBD.

[B] Gambling Disorder

How to recognize it: Gambling disorder is characterized by obsessive or habitual gambling behavior. It is the uncontrollable urge to gamble despite the gambling causing harm and taking a toll on the client's life (Mayo Clinic, 2022b). Clients who are not meeting their financial goals or are taking on debt due to gambling may be experiencing gambling disorder.

How to measure it:

Pathological Gambling	Strongly Disagree	Disagree	Disagree A Little	Agree A Little	Agree	Strongly Agree
I have trouble controlling my gambling.	1	2	3	4	5	6
I gamble to make relieve stress or make myself feel better.	1	2	3	4	5	6
I have to gamble with more and more money to keep it exciting.	1	2	3	4	5	6
I have committed an illegal act to get money for gambling.	1	2	3	4	5	6
I have borrowed money for gambling or have gambled on credit.	1	2	3	4	5	6
My gambling interferes with other aspects of my life (e.g., work, education, relationships).	1	2	3	4	5	6
I have hidden my gambling from people close to me.	1	2	3	4	5	6

How to address it: Gambling disorder also requires treatment beyond the scope of a financial planner. Clients with gambling disorder should seek help from a mental health professional or health care provider (Mayo Clinic, 2022a). Financial planners can help their client manage expectations about their experience when they seek help. In all likelihood, the trained professional will ask the client questions about their gambling habits, review their medical information, and do a health assessment. Treatments include therapy (i.e., behavioral therapy or cognitive behavioral therapy), medication, and self-help groups such as Gamblers Anonymous. Relapse is certainly possible, so you can help your clients stay accountable for their recovery after treatment and encourage them to seek additional treatment if a relapse occurs or seems imminent.

[C] Hoarding Disorder

How to recognize it: Hoarding can be recognized by the client having difficulty discarding or parting with objects, goods, or animals over time which can lead to excess accumulation, clutter, and dangerous living conditions. Hoarding behavior may be difficult for financial

in the client's home or office or if the client has a partner who brings the disorder to the financial planner's attention. Unless the client couple both have a hoarding disorder, hoarding can cause tremendous conflict and marital problems since it impacts the non-hoarding spouse's living environment. Hoarding can begin as early as age 11-15, and typically becomes more severe with age (Mayo Clinic, 2023b). The signs of hoarding include: disorganized piles or stacks of items, cluttered or obstructed walking and living spaces, buildup of food and trash, distress or problems functioning inside the home, conflict with family and friends who try to help with removing clutter, difficulty organizing items, and losing important documents. Hoarding behavior can also be transferred across family generations, so if their parent or other close family member exhibited hoarding behavior, it is possible the client may be more likely to exhibit hoarding behavior too.

How to measure it:

Compulsive Hoarding	Strongly Disagree	Disagree	Disagree A Little	Agree A Little	Agree	Strongly Agree
I have trouble throwing things away, even if they aren't worth much.	1	2	3	4	5	6
My living space is cluttered with things I don't use.	1	2	3	4	5	6
Throwing something away makes me feel like I am losing a part of myself.	1	2	3	4	5	6
I feel emotionally attached to my possessions.	1	2	3	4	5	6
My possessions give me a sense of safety and security.	1	2	3	4	5	6
I have trouble using my living space because of clutter.	1	2	3	4	5	6
I feel irresponsible if I get rid of an item.	1	2	3	4	5	6
I hide my need to hold on to items from others.	1	2	3	4	5	6

How to address it: Hoarding creates many problems including physical safety issues due to risk of a client falling and injuring themselves, unsanitary conditions, and fire hazards. Again, financial planners are

the client to seek help from a qualified mental health professional. The mental health professional may use psychotherapy (i.e., talk therapy) or cognitive behavioral therapy to treat the disorder (Mayo Clinic, 2023a). Medication may also be prescribed if anxiety or depression are also present. It may also be necessary to hire professionals to remove the clutter, professionally clean the home, and conduct any repairs that may have been neglected due to lack of access issues.

[D] Financial Dependence (a.k.a. Affluenza)

How to recognize it: Financial dependence occurs when someone relies on another person for non-work income. This reliance can lead to intense feelings of fear of being cut off, anxiety, shame, anger, and resentment (Klontz et al., 2012). It is possible for your client to be financially dependent on another person or it is possible for another person to be financially dependent on your client (i.e., financial enabling). Financial dependence can lead to negative feelings for both the dependent person and the person providing the funds. Financial planners are in a uniquely strong position to recognize the signs of financial dependence. Receiving large gifts or a significant stream of income gifted to your client could indicate your client's financial dependence. If your client wants to build gifts or income from another person into their financial plan, they are displaying signs of financial dependence.

How to measure it:

Financial Dependence	Strongly Disagree	Disagree	Disagree A Little	Agree A Little	Agree	Strongly Agree
I feel like the money I get comes with strings attached	1	2	3	4	5	6
I often feel resentment or anger related to the money I receive.	1	2	3	4	5	6
A significant portion of my income comes from money I do nothing to earn (e.g., trust fund, compensation payments).	1	2	3	4	5	6
I have significant fear or anxiety that I will be cut off from my non-work income.	1	2	3	4	5	6
The non-work income I receive seems to stifle my motivation, passion, cre-	1	2	3	4	5	6

How to address it: Although it may be helpful to involve a mental health professional, family therapist, or financial therapist in financial dependency situations, there are some steps that financial planners can take to help their clients set better boundaries. Financial planners can broach the topic of the problematic relationship and encourage the client to set boundaries, especially if the client feels the money is being received with strings attached. Additionally, the financial planner can partner with the client to develop a plan to work towards financial self-sufficiency.

[E] Financial Enabling

How to recognize it: Financial enabling occurs when a client sends money to another individual on a regular basis, even at the own cost of their own financial plan and financial goals. Financial enabling is characterized by an inability to turn down another person's request for financial assistance even if they feel taken advantage of financially (Klontz et al., 2012).

How to measure it:

Financial Enabling	Strongly Disagree	Disagree	Disagree A Little	Agree A Little	Agree	Strongly Agree
I give money to others even though I can't afford it.	1	2	3	4	5	6
I have trouble saying "no" to requests for money from family or friends.	1	2	3	4	5	6
I sacrifice my financial well-being for the sake of others.	1	2	3	4	5	6
People take advantage of me around money.	1	2	3	4	5	6
I lend money without making clear arrangements for repayment.	1	2	3	4	5	6
I often find myself feeling resentment or anger after giving money to others.	1	2	3	4	5	6

How to address it: It is particularly important for the financial planner to address the financial enabling if the client's own financial plan and goals are being harmed by another person's dependence. It is still important

enabling is unhealthy. Financial planners can work with their clients to find healthier methods of supporting their loved ones. Financial planners can also help in situations like this by calculating how much support the clients can afford to give. Financial planners can help the client develop boundaries around the support they provide, and they may even wish to offer boundary-building workshops as a benefit to their clients (Lurtz, 2020).

[F] Money Scripts

According to Klontz's definition, money scripts are beliefs that people have about money (Klontz et al., 2011). It is possible to have hundreds of different money scripts. Each person will have a different and unique set of money scripts which started forming at an early age. Below are a few examples of money scripts that are widely held:

- I believe that money is inherently good.

- I believe that money is not worth pursuing because it will create more problems that it will solve.

- I believe that having money creates more opportunities for conflict.

- I believe that you should never talk about money.

- I believe that I deserve to have money.

- I believe that money will add more meaning to my life.

Money scripts can impact a client's financial behavior. Financial planners can gain a deeper understanding of their clients' beliefs and behaviors by identifying their underlying money beliefs.

Money scripts can typically be categorized into 4 different categories: money avoidance, money worship, money status, and money vigilance (Klontz et al., 2011). The money belief questions from the Klontz Money Script Inventory for each of the 4 categories of money scripts are listed in Figure 5.1 below. These statements may be helpful as a point of reference as you learn more about your clients to help you identify their

Figure 5.1. Klontz Money Script Inventory

Money Avoidance

- I do not deserve a lot of money when others have less than me.
- Rich people are greedy.
- It is not okay to have more than you need.
- People get rich by taking advantage of others.
- I do not deserve money.
- Good people should not care about money.
- It is hard to be rich and be a good person.
- Most rich people do not deserve their money.
- There is virtue in living with less money.
- The less money you have, the better life is.
- Money corrupts people.
- Being rich means you no longer fit in with old friends and family.
- The rich take their money for granted.
- You cannot be rich and trust what people want from you.
- It is hard to accept financial gifts from others.

Money Worship

- Things would get better if I had more money.
- More money will make you happier.
- There will never be enough money.
- It is hard to be poor and happy.
- You can never have enough money.
- Money is power.
- I will never be able to afford the things I really want in life.
- Money would solve all my problems.
- Money buys freedom.
- If you have money, someone will try to take it away from you.
- You can't trust people around money.

Money Status

- Most poor people do not deserve to have money.
- You can have love or money, but not both.
- I will not buy something unless it is new (e.g., car, house).
- Poor people are lazy.
- Money is what gives life meaning.
- Your self-worth equals your net worth.
- If something is not considered the "best," it is not worth buying.
- People are only as successful as the amount of money they earn.
- It is okay to keep secrets from your partner around money.
- As long as you live a good life you will always have enough money.
- Rich people have no reason to be unhappy.
- If you are good, your financial needs will be taken care of.
- If someone asked me how much I earned, I would probably tell them I earn more than I actually do.

Money Vigilance

- You should not tell others how much money you have or make.
- It is wrong to ask others how much money they have or make.
- Money should be saved not spent.
- It is important to save for a rainy day.
- People should work for their money and not be given financial handouts.
- If someone asked me how much I earned, I would probably tell them I earn less than I actually do.
- You should always look for the best deal before buying something, even if it takes more time.
- If you cannot pay cash for something, you should not buy it.
- It is not polite to talk about money.
- I would be a nervous wreck if I did not have money saved for an emergency.

5.4 STRATEGIES TO OVERCOME PSYCHOLOGICAL BARRIERS OBSERVED IN CLIENTS

There are several ways a practitioner can overcome clients' psychological barriers, as illustrated in Figure 5.2.

Figure 5.2. Goals and Tools to Overcome Clients' Psychological Barriers

1   Assessments

- Goal: Use reliable and validated scales (i.e., questionnaires) during the data gathering phase of planning to determine what psychological barriers your clients may need help with.
- Tools: Consumer Financial Protection Bureau's financial well-being scale, Furnham Money Beliefs and Behavior Scale, Klontz Money Behavior Inventory, Klontz Money Script Inventory, and the Money Sanity/Pathology Scale.

2   Motivational Interviewing

- Goal: To make clients aware of their own money scripts and problematic financial behaviors.
- Tools: The Understanding Motivational Interviewing guide found at motivationalinterviewing.org.

3   Nudges and Framing

- Goal: Help the client feel more comfortabe taking action by posing a question or a situation in different ways. Typically, positive framing will make a client feel more comfortable.
- Tools: Frame estate planning as "legacy planning" instead of "estate planning." Legacy has a positive connocation whereas most people view estate planning as negative, painful, and time consuming; https://www.kitces.com/blog/behavioral-biases-nudges-smart-heuristics-behavioral-coaching-interventions-hierarchy/.

4   Checklists

- Goal: Make financial plan implementation easier for the client by creating checklists for the client to use. This makes the recommendations very clear and progress is easy to track. This is particularly useful for clients that feel less motivated to take action.
- Tools: https://www.kitces.com/blog/fppathfinder-financial-planning-checklists-and-flowcharts-due-diligence/.

5   Team-Based Interventions

- Goal: Work with additional professionals such as mental health professionals, therapists, and financial therapists to address client needs that cannot be addressed by a financial planner's skillset alone.
- Tools: See Chapter 14 for more detailed instructions on how to build a referral network.

6   Financial Education

- Goal: Bring about change by bringing information and awareness to the client about the psychological barriers they are experiencing and how they can overcome them.
- Tools: *The Psychology of Financial Planning*; All of the information in this chapter, and more broadly, this book.

5.5 CLIENT PSYCHOLOGY BARRIERS: DO'S AND DON'TS

The left-hand side of the chart below summarizes some of the key steps financial planners can take to talk to clients about their psychological barriers. The column on the right contains steps that should be avoided as they can be detrimental in your pursuit of building a connection with your client.

Do	Don't
• Do understand how clients financial socialization, the development of their financial values, can impact their money beliefs and financial behavior.	• Don't try to address pathological financial behaviors without the help of qualified mental health professionals trained in therepeutic techniques and interventions.
• Do explore your own money scripts and your clients' money scripts.	• Don't assume that every person involved in a family business transition will act with the family's best interests in mind (Fredo Effect).
• Do use the strategies in this chapter (assessments, motivational interviewing, nudges, checklists, team-based interventions, and financial education) to help your clients overcome their barriers.	

References

Black, D. W. (2007). A review of compulsive buying disorder. *World Psychiatry, 6*(1), 14-18.

Klontz, B., Britt, S. L., Archuleta, K. L. and Klontz, T. (2012). Disordered money behaviors: Development of the Klontz money behavior inventory. *Journal of Financial Therapy, 3*(1), 17-42.

Klontz, B., Britt, S. L. and Mentzer, J. (2011). Money beliefs and financial behaviors: Development of the Klontz Money Script Inventory. *Journal of Financial Therapy, 2*(1), 1-22.

Lurtz, M. (2020, May 20). Border wars: Helping clients set financial (and emotional) boundaries to avoid enabling dependent family members. *Kitces.com.* https://www.kitces.com/blog/financial-enabling-true-boundary-limits-consequences-enforcement-dave-jetson-advisor-client/.

Mayo Clinic. (2022a, June 18). *Compulsive gambling: Diagnosis and treatment.* Mayoclinic.org. https://www.mayoclinic.org/diseases-conditions/compulsive-gambling/diagnosis-treatment/drc-20355184

Mayo Clinic. (2022b, June 18). *Compulsive gambling: Symptoms and causes*. Mayoclinic.org. https://www.mayoclinic.org/diseases-conditions/compulsive-gambling/symptoms-causes/syc-20355178.

Mayo Clinic. (2023a, January 26). *Hoarding disorder: Diagnosis and treatment*. Mayoclinic.org. https://www.mayoclinic.org/diseases-conditions/hoarding-disorder/diagnosis-treatment/drc-20356062.

Mayo Clinic. (2023b, January 26). *Hoarding disorder: Symptoms and causes*. Mayoclinic.org. https://www.mayoclinic.org/diseases-conditions/hoarding-disorder/symptoms-causes/syc-20356056.

Sages, R. and Chatterjee, S. (2022). Client psychology barriers in the financial planning process and strategies for overcoming them. In S. Chatterjee, S. Lutter and D. Yeske (Eds.), *The Psychology of Financial Planning* (pp. 76-93). Certified Financial Planner Board of Standards, Inc.

Chapter 6

Building the Client's Motivation for Achieving Their Financial Goals

6.1 INTRODUCTION

Only a small proportion of clients that seek out a financial advisor are ready to take action. You can find much greater success in working with clients and having clients implement recommendations if you understand how to help a client increase their motivation to improve their financial behavior and financial decisions. Unsurprisingly, this is much easier said than done.

Not every financial planner is interested in taking the extra step to help their clients find the motivation to implement the planning recommendations. For some, ensuring their technical expertise is displayed by developing optimal recommendations is enough. However, integrated financial planners go beyond just the financial details. An integrated planner addresses both interior finance (client's emotional relationships with

> **Integrated Financial Planner**
>
> A financial planner who addresses both interior finance (client's emotional relationships with money) and exterior finance (traditional financial concerns).

financial planners take a broader perspective, seeking to understand their client's relationship with money and how that may create barriers to implementation.

6.2 BUILDING A CLIENT'S MOTIVATION IN PRACTICE

It can be very frustrating to go through the majority of the financial planning process only to get stuck at the implementation phase because the client does not want to take the next steps. This can be displayed in several different ways. Sometimes, clients disagree with the recommendation and refuse to implement it for that reason. Other times, the client may agree that the recommendation is helpful and necessary, but never contacts the estate attorney or follows up with the long-term care specialist despite being reminded in every meeting.

The list below underscores some of the key ideas from Chapter 6: Building the Client's Motivation for Achieving Their Financial Goals in *The Psychology of Financial Planning* (Kahler, 2022). These items are particularly relevant for practitioners who are trying to help clients find their motivation to make meaningful change.

- The utility of money is to support our search for meaning in life. Money itself cannot provide meaning.

- Although feelings about money may be temporary, the consequences of behaviors and decisions they inspire typically endure.

- Awareness of a problem is rarely enough to inspire behavior change or motivation.

- The most impactful motivations are intrinsic (coming from within a client). Advisors can help clients explore problematic money behaviors in a safe and non-judgmental setting, allowing space for the internal work a client must do to evaluate their barriers to action.

- Problematic behaviors can rarely be addressed quickly. It will take time and a high level of skill to address. Additionally, you may wish to partner with a Certified Financial Therapist™ or

- It is important to recognize that problematic financial behaviors are often rooted in financial trauma. Note the circumstances below which can often be a source of financial trauma that should be explored, as illustrated in Figure 6.1.

Figure 6.1. Financial Trauma

- Financial planners should recognize that change is stressful for clients. Susan Bradley lists nine different common emotions and behaviors that can accompany change. Financial planners can help their clients by normalizing their emotions when they go through these transitions. Planners can also build trust and rapport by acknowledging the client's feelings and acknowledging the challenges the client is facing. Remember, empathy is very important for clients trying to change a behavior (see Chapter 15)

Figure 6.2. Common Feelings Related to Financial Transactions

- Trauma can be a root cause of disordered or problematic financial behaviors. Trauma, typically experienced during childhood, can lead to harmful money scripts which ultimately impact how people behave with their money (see Chapter 4). The behavioral and emotional signs of trauma are identified below. If you notice these signs in your clients, consider partnering with or referring them to a trained mental health professional for help addressing the root cause of harmful financial behavior.

Figure 6.3. Behavioral and Emotional Signs of Financial Trauma

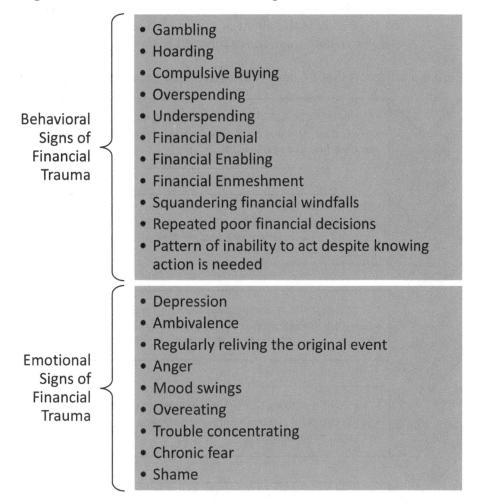

Behavioral Signs of Financial Trauma

- Gambling
- Hoarding
- Compulsive Buying
- Overspending
- Underspending
- Financial Denial
- Financial Enabling
- Financial Enmeshment
- Squandering financial windfalls
- Repeated poor financial decisions
- Pattern of inability to act despite knowing action is needed

Emotional Signs of Financial Trauma

- Depression
- Ambivalence
- Regularly reliving the original event
- Anger
- Mood swings
- Overeating
- Trouble concentrating
- Chronic fear
- Shame

6.3 ASSESSING A CLIENT'S READINESS TO CHANGE

The Transtheoretical Model of Behavior Change (introduced in Chapter 2) describes the stages that clients go through while moving towards making long-term changes to their behavior. When assessing a client's readiness for change, it is important to be present and truly listen to the client. The active listening techniques described in Chapter 13 will be very helpful as you try to determine the client's stage of change.

Figure 6.4 describes the signals you can look for that might indicate a client is in a particular stage of change. Once you have identified which stage of change the client is in, you can identify the best strategies to employ to help them move forward to the next stage of change.

Figure 6.4. Signals that a Client is in a Particular Stage of Change

Precontemplation	• Clients don't believe there is a problem (ignorance/denial). • Signs: Overspending, financial enabling, excess and unwise risk-taking, avoiding financial realities, etc.
Contemplation	• The client starts to entertain the idea of their behavior being a problem. • Signs: The client asks for new information from the planner about the outcome of their current behavior or alternative behaviors that they could adopt.
Preparation	• The client makes a commitment to changing their behavior. • Signs: The client starts creating a plan of action to make the change; the client asks for advice, information, and direction from the financial planner.
Action	• The client is working through the process of actually changing their behavior. • Signs: The client is implementing recommendations; the problematic behavior is changing or diminishing.
Maintenance	• The client is practicing the new behavior(s) and is learning to make the new behavior a regular part of their lives. • Signs: The behavior change is being maintained (if relapse occurs, support and encourage the client to continue working towards behavior change)

Grubman, Bollerud and Holland (2011) recommend assessing a client's readiness to change by asking the following questions.

Figure 6.5. Assessing a Client's Readiness Questions

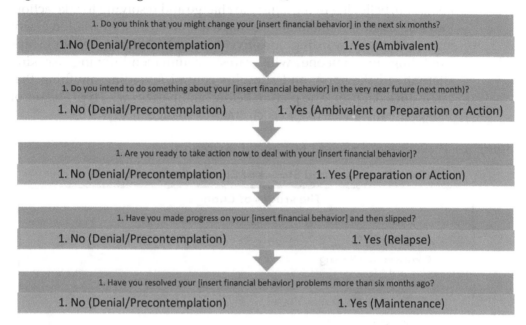

6.4 BUILDING MOTIVATION: INTERVENTIONS

While assessing the client's readiness for change, there are a number of approaches that can be very detrimental to clients that are moving towards changing their behavior. Shaming or manipulating the client will damage the working relationship and may even move the client further away from being ready to change. Lecturing and providing more education and data are also unlikely to solicit the desired effect.

Instead, it is typically much more effective to utilize strategies that can help a client build their intrinsic motivation. For this, we can turn once again to TTM. There are 10 processes of change in the TTM which explain how (rather than when) a person changes behavior (Xiao et al., 2004). In the precontemplation stage, the most effective processes of change are consciousness raising, dramatic relief, and environmental reevaluation. Consciousness raising increases information and awareness about the behavior and the need for change, and dramatic relief means expressing emotions about the problem. Environmental reevaluation highlights the problem's effect on the situation. Self-reevaluation, assessing

contemplation stage. The preparation stage should emphasize self-liberation, believing in the ability to change and resolving to take action. Individuals in the maintenance stage should focus on reinforcement management (rewarding positive change), helping relationships (confiding in someone who cares), counterconditioning (seeking alternative behaviors), and stimulus control (avoiding anything that can induce relapse). The picture below summarizes which processes of change are most effective in each stage of change in TTM.

Figure 6.6. Processes and Stages of Change Integration

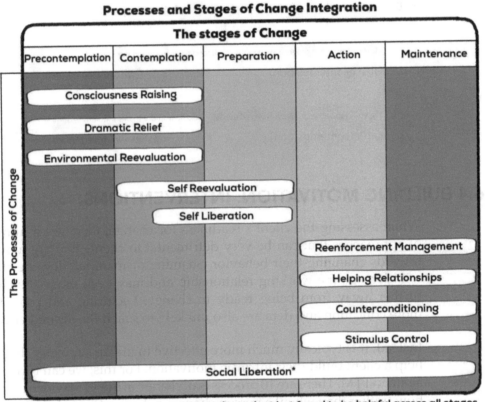

6.5 THREE BASIC CONDITIONS FOR CHANGE

A person's decisional balance and self-efficacy also play a role in their

relative weight of the pros and cons of changing behavior (Prochaska et al., 1996). This will be different for each client. Self-efficacy is a person's belief in their capacity to change behavior (Xiao et al., 2004).

There are three conditions that must be met before a client is ready to change: perceived *need* to change, perceived *ability* to change, and the client's *readiness* to change (Kahler et al., 2007). A client's decisional balance will impact perceived need to change, and a person's level of self-efficacy will impact their perceived ability to change.

You can think of the following as a checklist to ensure each of the three conditions are met:

- Perceived Need to Change

- Perceived Ability to Change

- Client's Readiness to Change

If any of these conditions are not met, you can focus your attention accordingly and address the missing condition in a deliberate way.

6.6 THREE QUESTIONS FOR AMBIVALENT CLIENTS

Lawson and his colleagues (2017) suggested questions for clients ambivalent to change. These questions are not complicated and are easy to ask. These questions are most effective for clients that at least know behavior change is needed (e.g., they know their portfolio will be depleted within 5 years if they continue spending at the current level), but they do not yet want to make the change nor do they have the motivation to make the change (i.e., they do not want to decrease their portfolio distributions and make cuts to their lifestyle despite knowing they will run out of money in a few years). The three questions are:

- Tell me why you want to make this change.

- Talk about what you need to do to succeed in making this change.

- Please say more about why making this change is so important

6.7 MOTIVATION: DO'S AND DON'TS

The left-hand side of the chart below summarizes some of the key steps financial planners can take to talk to clients about their financial motivations. The column on the right contains steps that should be avoided as they can be detrimental in your pursuit of building a connection with your client.

Do	Don't
• Do understand the 6 stages of change and try to evaluate which stage of change your client is in.	• Don't assume raising a client's awareness of a problematic behavior will be sufficient for behavior change to occur.
• Do use active listening techniques (see Chapter 13) to find and understand the barriers to action clients are facing.	• Don't shame clients or confront them in an attempt to change behavior. This may have the opposite effect you intend.
• Do ask open questions and statements like "Tell me more...."	• Don't lecture or scold clients for their behavior
• Do identify and explore the client's money scripts.	• Don't provide more data to try to get clients to change behavior.
• Do examine your own money scripts and financial trauma before working with your clients on theirs. Recognize how your own experiences may shape and influence your work with clients.	• Don't set deadlines or give ultimatums.
• Do consider working with a financial therapist to do your own internal work.	• Don't manipulate the client or people around them.
• Do give yourself permission to move slowly as you begin learning how to help clients build their motivation.	• Don't warn about possible consequences.
	• Don't ask questions like, "What is standing in the way of you getting this done."

Resource List

The need for behavior change is a tremendously difficult challenge to address with clients, especially if the client is still in an early stage of change. The resource list is a starting point of additional resources, exercises, and tools that may be helpful in your work with clients trying to change a behavior.

- George Kinder's 3 Questions

- Money Quotient

- The Wheel of Life

- Financial Satisfaction and Life Transitions

- *Facilitating Financial Health* (Klontz et al., 2016)

- The Money Egg

- The Money Atom

- Dow Jones Money Timeline

- Financial Integration Inventory

- Life Aspirations Exercise

- The Money Dialogue

References

Grubman, J., Bollerud, K. and Holland, C. R. (2011). Motivating and helping the overspending client: A stages-of-change model. *Journal of Financial Planning*, 24(3), 60-67.

Kahler, R. (2022). Building the client's motivation for achieving their financial goals. In S. Chatterjee, S. Lutter and D. Yeske (Eds.), *The Psychology of Financial Planning* (ch. 6). Certified Financial Planner Board of Standards, Inc.

Kahler, R., Klontz, T. and Klontz, B. (2007). Helping clients change: 21st century tools from a 19th century fable. *Journal of Financial Planning*, 20(4), 62-67.

Klontz, B., Kahler, R. and Klontz, T. (2016). *Facilitating Financial Health: Tools for Financial Planners, Coaches, and Therapists, 2nd Edition* (2nd ed.). The National Underwriter Company.

Lawson, D. R., Klontz, B. and T. Klontz. (2017). Integrating behavioral finance, financial psychology, and financial therapy into the 6-step financial planning process. *Journal of Financial Planning 30*(7), 48-55.

Prochaska, J., Redding, C. and Evers, K. (1996). The transtheoretical model and stages of change. In K. Glanz, F. Lewis and B. Rimer (Eds.), *Health Behavior and Health Education: Theory, Research, and Practice* (2nd ed., pp. 60-84). San Francisco: Jossey-Bass.

Xiao, J. J., Newman, B. M., Prochaska, J. M., Leon, B., Bassett, R. and Johnson, J. L. (2004). Applying the transtheoretical model of change to debt reducing behavior. *Financial Counseling and Planning, 15*(2), 89-100.

Chapter 7

Examining Couple and Family Financial Transparency

7.1 INTRODUCTION

As a financial planner, it is essential to ensure the information and data you are using to build a financial plan is accurate and complete. It is not ethical for a CERTIFIED FINANCIAL

Financial Transparency
The open and honest disclosure of one's finances.

PLANNER™ professional to provide recommendations based on known false or incomplete information. As such, financial planners should strive to ensure clients are being completely transparent with you and your colleagues. As defined by Koochel et al. (2020), financial transparency is "the open and honest disclosure of one's finances." It is important to cultivate financial transparency not only between a financial planner and their client but also between the members of the household themselves.

7.2 FINANCIAL TRANSPARENCY IN PRACTICE

The items below are important concepts from Chapter 7: Examining
Couple and Family Financial Transparency in The Psychology of Financial

Planning (Koochel and Lurtz, 2022) that are particularly relevant to financial planners.

- Clients are not always honest. This dishonesty can take many shapes and forms. Sometimes the client may withhold the truth from their partner, sometimes their financial planner. Sometimes they are withholding the truth from themselves.

- Depending on the situation, you may wish to consult with other financial planning or mental health professionals.

7.3 WHY DO CLIENTS LIE (ACCORDING TO THEORY)

Before examining how to address transparency issues, it may be useful to understand *why* some clients may have difficulty being transparent with you. The list below describes the explanations that various theories offer for why a client may not with to be completely honest. For a more complete description of each theory, refer to Chapter 7: Examining Couple and Family Financial Transparency in *The Psychology of Financial Planning* (Koochel and Lurtz, 2022). To summarize the points in Figure 7.1, some of the primary reasons people lie are because they believe it benefits them in some way or they have learned to behave in a dishonest way, either through experiences in their past or from watching a parent's behavior or absorbing values from their social system.

Figure 7.1. Primary Reasons why Clients Lie

Conflict Theory	The foundation of conflict stems from competition for scarce resources.
	Clients may lie in situations where they can gain power or resources (money) from doing so.
	Understanding the power dynamics at play in a client interaction may help you understand why someone is being dishonest.
	Conflict where one person uses a power imbalance to their advantage is unhealthy.
Social Exchange Theory	The foundation of conflict stems from operating in a cost and reward system.
	People will be dishonest when they perceive the rewards (money, social approval, respect, compliance) will outweigh the costs (anything unpleasant or undesirable).
	Note that different clients will value certain rewards and costs differently based on their own value system. This explains why people in similar situations may behave differently.
Couples and Finance Theory	Every situation and interaction is impacted by a web of interrelated and separate systems.
	The relationship and the financial processes of the couple/family are both separate but interrelated systems that financial planners need to understand for each client.
	Financial inputs, financial management, marital quality, and how the couple interacts with each other are major factors that impact the goal congruence and conflict within the couple.
Family Financial Socialization Theory	Financial behavior (including financial transparency) is influenced heavily by the financial attitudes, values, and behaviors of families and people within one's social system. This socialization begins during childhood but continues over time throughout the lifespan.
	Lying about financial matters, or just dishonesty in general, may be a transfered behavior based on attitudes and values someone was exposed to or socialized growing up.
Social Learning Theory	Financial behavior (including financial transparency) is influenced heavily by what is learned or witnessed within families and society.
	Learning is not always intentional or conscious. Clients may not even be aware they are exibiting a learned behavior.
	Dishonesty may occur due to social pressures or perceived societal norms.
Communication Privacy Management	All people like to keep some information private. Disclosing private information can feel uncomfortable as it can cause feelings of vulnerability.

7.4 FINANCIAL TRANSPARENCY SCALE

The scale below was developed by Emily Koochel and her colleagues (2020) to help researchers and practitioners assess and measure a person's level of financial transparency in their relationship. The scale measures three dimensions: Financial Partnership, Financial Secrecy, and Financial Trust and Disclosure. Although it may not be appropriate to measure each and every client's financial transparency, this scale may be helpful to utilize during a client engagement if clients are seeking your guidance on building more financial transparency. It may also be appropriate to use after a lack of financial transparency has been observed or identified by the financial planner or the co-client (i.e., one of the spouses in the household). Of course, the clients need to consent to the use of the Financial Transparency Scale (see Figure 7.2) and should be willing participants in evaluating the couple's level of financial transparency.

Figure 7.2. Financial Transparency Scale

Please indicate how often the following occur between **you and your partner.**					
	Never	Seldom	Occasionally	Usually	Always
1. Discuss finances openly and honestly					
2. Review financial statements together (credit card statements, investment statements, etc.)					
3. Discuss how money should be spent					
4. Discuss how money should be saved					
5. Make savings goals for the future together					
6. Review credit reports together					
7. Discuss outstanding debts					

Please indicate how likely the following are to occur between **you and your partner.**

	Not at All Likely	Not Likely	Somewhat Likely	Likely	Very Likely
8. Review a current budget together					
9. Discuss spending habits					
10. Set long-term (more than 5 years) financial goals together					
11. Set short-term (less than 1 year) financial goals together					
12. Discuss family expenses					
13. Pay bills together					
14. Plan ahead for large purchases together					
15. Keep records of expenditures and income					
16. Prepare estate documents together (wills, trusts, powers of attorney, etc.)					
17. Discuss repayment of outstanding debt					
18. Discuss savings plans for retirement					

Please indicate how likely **you** are to do the following.

	Not at all Likely	Not Likely	Somewhat Likely	Likely	Very Likely
19. Lie to your partner about a financial transaction					
20. Lie about a purchase to your partner					
21. Keep a secret from your partner regarding spending					
22. Disclose all of your					

	Not at all Likely	Not Likely	Somewhat Likely	Likely	Very Likely
23. Trust your partner's financial judgment					
24. Trust your partner's financial management					
25. Disclose your earnings to your partner					
26. Disclose a bonus to your partner					

7.5 LEADING QUESTIONS FOR FINANCIAL PLANNING PRACTITIONERS

If using the scale does not feel authentic to your practice or your style of data gathering, another option would be to use leading questions during the initial consultation. These questions may also help you assess the need for exploring if there may be financial transparency issues at play. Koochel and Lurtz (2022) suggest the following questions:

- What is your current spending plan?

- When do you typically discuss your finances with your spouse/partner.

- What is your earliest memory of money or most significant memory of money from as early as you remember?

7.6 EXAMINING TRANSPARENCY: DO'S AND DON'T

The chart below can help you determine which steps to take and which steps to avoid when helping your clients to achieve financial transparency.

Do	Don't
• Do encourage open and honest conversation and strive for greater financial transparency between all members of the engagement.	• Don't respond to clients with negativity or platitudes when a financial secret ot a lie has been exposed.
• Do understand that clients who are dishonest are likely experiencing shame, guilt, fear, anger, sadness, and many other emotions that are creating an unwillingness to be completely transparent.	• Don't assume that someone who has engaged your services is automatically ready to be completely open about their finances.
• Do use phrases like "tell me more about what is going on."	• Don't use phrases like "why didn't you tell me" or "why would you keep this from me when I'm your financial planner."
• Do respect a client's boundaries while probing for more information.	• Don't cast shame or guilt on clients who have been dishonest or lied by omission.
• Do move the conversation towards something that is actionable for the client.	• Don't automatically assume you are your client's only financial planner. If you discover your client has multiple planners, it may be a clue you may not be privy to all of their financial information.
• Do build trust by accepting information without casting shame, blame, or guilt on a client	• Don't tackle issues that are out of your scope of practice.
• Do examine the financial flash point, the origin of each partner's money beliefs, to help you uncover problematic and beneficial patterns and behaviors.	

References

Koochel, E. and Lurtz, M. (2022). Examining Couple and Family Financial Transparency. In S. Chatterjee, S. Lutter and D. Yeske (Eds.), *The Psychology of Financial Planning* (ch. 7). Certified Financial Planner Board of Standards, Inc.

Koochel, E. E., Markham, M. S., Crawford, D. W. and Archuleta, K. L. (2020). Financial

Chapter 8

Mediating Financial Conflict

8.1 INTRODUCTION

Although financial planners are not necessarily formally trained to deal with conflict, inevitably every planner will witness financial conflict of some form within their practice. Conflict is a serious difference between ideas, interests, or needs (Collins Dictionary, n.d.). Conflict is natural in almost every setting because conflict stems from different perspectives. No two people have exactly the same perspective on every aspect of life.

Conflict can occur between the financial planner and the client, between members of a client household, between colleagues at the financial planning firm, or a combination of all of the above.

> **Conflict**
>
> Conflict is a serious difference between ideas, interests, or needs.

Conflict can occur for a wide variety of reasons, and it can range in severity from a small disagreement to issues that can completely end relationships.

Conflict can be very uncomfortable. In the moment, it can be difficult to determine how to address the conflict appropriately. It can also be difficult to accept that not all conflict can or will be overcome. Regardless of the reason and the severity of the conflict, there are steps financial planners can take to help address conflict in a healthy way and move

There are certain communication techniques that are particularly useful when working to resolve conflict. The nonviolent communication process (discussed in Chapter 3) is an excellent starting point for addressing financial conflicts (The Center for Nonviolent Communication ["CNVC"], n.d.). Financial planners should also use empathy, reframing, reflective listening, and assertive messaging to address conflict situations (Asebedo and Purdon, 2018). These communication techniques are discussed in more detail in Chapter 13.

8.2 MEDIATING CONFLICT IN PRACTICE

In practice, conflict on some level is probably a daily or almost daily occurrence. It is natural for people to disagree. Remember, it is not going to be appropriate for you to insert yourself into your client's conflict. However, your clients may bring a disagreement to you, or a conflict situation may arise during your meetings or encounters with clients. Conflict that you encounter in practice will also range dramatically in severity. Some disagreements may just be based on a misunderstanding and can be resolved by asking a few thoughtful, clarifying questions. Other conflicts are ultimately impassable and will lead to divorce or dissolution of the client-planner relationship. However, there is a vast middle ground where financial planners can provide a lot of value. Regardless of the severity of the conflict, there are steps financial planners can take to hopefully reach a positive outcome, but these steps can also serve to minimize the damage conflict can cause.

The list below summarizes some of the key points from Chapter 8: Mediating Financial Conflict in *The Psychology of Financial Planning* (Lutter and Koochel, 2022).

- When it comes to conflict, perceptions can be more important than reality. If conflict is perceived, conflict is definitely present. Additionally, conflict can occur due to perceived issues even if the perception does not match reality. For example, imagine Partner A perceives that Partner B is spending frivolously at the grocery store due to the fact that the average grocery spending in their budget has increased by 20%. In reality, Partner B is dedicating a lot of time and energy to comparing prices and shopping on sale, but the prices on groceries in their area have increased dramatically and only so much can be done to combat that. In this situation, there is still a conflict even though perceptions don't match the reality.

- The earlier the conflict can be recognized and addressed, the more likely the conflict can be controlled or deescalated.

- There are a wide variety of causes for conflict. Regardless of the cause, conflict is natural and should be expected.

8.3 RECOGNIZING CONFLICT

The items below are important signals that may indicate some conflict may be occurring between your clients. Although the list is not comprehensive, it should provide some guidance as to which signs you should look for when determining if a financial conflict is present in your work with your clients. Conflict cues can come in three different forms: verbal cues, nonverbal cues, and physiological cues. Cues from one, two, or all three categories may be present.

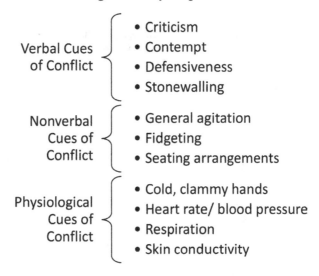

Verbal Cues of Conflict
- Criticism
- Contempt
- Defensiveness
- Stonewalling

Nonverbal Cues of Conflict
- General agitation
- Fidgeting
- Seating arrangements

Physiological Cues of Conflict
- Cold, clammy hands
- Heart rate/ blood pressure
- Respiration
- Skin conductivity

8.4 SOURCES OF CONFLICT

Figure 8.1 illustrates some of the primary root causes that may be creating financial conflict. Once you've recognized a conflict may exist based on the signals described previously, the next step is to investigate the root cause of the conflict (if appropriate). Important considerations

Figure 8.1. Root Causes of Conflict

Differing Values	• Remain impartial; do not show a preference for a certain value over another. • Converse with clients about their values as part of the data gathering process. • Evaluate client's preferences for accumulating financial assets versus non-financial assets; discuss any incongrencies between clients.
Spending Styles	• A wide disparity in partners' credit scores can indicate a spending style conflict. • Know that spending style conflict tends to be more intense if the wife is seen as the spender than if the husband is perceived as the spender (Britt et al, 2017). • Engage in a conversation about each partner's perceived current spending relative to ideal spending. Correct any misperceptions that may be present.
Power Imbalances	• Differences in income can create power imbalances or perceived power imbalances in couples. • Even couples that make "joint" decisions may not have equal decision-making power. • Ensure both partners have an opportunity to express their feelings about a decision,
Gender Differences	• Traditional gender roles have diminished in Western countries. • Even so, be aware that marital conflict increases when wives earn more than their husbands (Britt et al., 2010).
Financial Infidelity	• Financial infidelity, committing financial deception against a partner (NEFE, 2018) can range from the seemingly benign to severe.
Financial Transparency	• Financial transparency requires trust. • Time is key in developing both trust and transparency.
Holistic Well-Being	• Consider using measures of psychological health (i.e., anxiety, depression) during the data gathering process.

8.5 CONFLICT STYLES

Sarah Asebedo and Emily Purdon (2018) have outlined five different styles of conflict. The five styles are laid out in Figure 8.2 indicating the level of assertiveness and cooperativeness demonstrated in each style.

Figure 8.2. Five Styles of Conflict

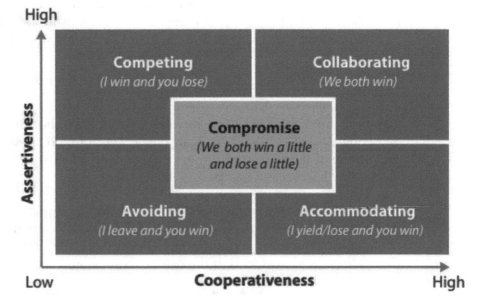

Avoiding. Low Cooperativeness, Low Assertiveness.

Conflict avoiders may prefer to avoid conflict because it feels easier. Avoiders prefer to back away from a conflict or ignore the problem, hoping the problem will go away or the conflict will resolve itself. Someone may also prefer to avoid a conflict to protect their feelings if they feel they have less decision-making power and will ultimately not be factored into a couple's decision-making process.

Appropriate When: Avoiding can be appropriate when the conflict is relatively minor or when a person needs additional time to think or process. Avoiding may also be appropriate if the timing is off and there is a better time in the near future to address the conflict.

Accommodating. High Cooperativeness, Low Assertiveness.

Conflict accommodators will prioritize the needs of others over their own needs. This is often done with the goal of "keeping the peace," but this prevents a true resolution to the conflict from being found.

Appropriate When: Accommodating is appropriate when you are in the wrong or if you have made a mistake. It may also be appropriate in isolated instances when an important relationship is at stake. Accommodating consistently and frequently is rarely appropriate or healthy.

Competing. Low Cooperativeness, High Assertiveness.

Conflict competitors try to gain power and intimidate the other person or people in the conflict. This can create confrontational situations. This is one of the riskiest and most dangerous conflict styles as it can irreparably harm relationships.

Appropriate When: Competing can make sense in urgent situations when quick decisions need to be made. This may occur in a crisis situation or when an unpopular decision needs to be implemented. Competing could also work if the conflict is small and the relationship is unlikely to be harmed.

Collaborating. High Cooperativeness, High Assertiveness.

Conflict collaborators can have a difficult task. It can take more initial effort to find creative solutions where the needs of parties can be met. It can also take skillful communication to navigate a conflict in a manner where the conflict can be approached in a sufficiently calm manner to discuss solutions. Underlying concerns need to be identified and time needs to be invested to understand the other party's views. However, the time invested is always worthwhile if a resolution can be found for both parties, the relationship may become stronger and more trusting as a result of the collaboration process.

Appropriate When: Collaborating is always appropriate, if possible. However, it is possible that a true win-win resolution may not be possible in every situation.

Compromising. Medium Cooperativeness, Medium Assertiveness.

Conflict compromisers are willing to sacrifice some of their goals put aside some of their needs if the other party is willing to do the same. The process takes time, but it can help to preserve the relationship while still reaching a satisfactory outcome for all parties.

<u>Appropriate When</u>: If a solution cannot be found through collaborating, compromise is the next best alternative. However, every effort should be made to find a collaborative solution before resorting to a compromise as a compromise can still result in goals and needs not being met in the long-term.

8.6 CONFLICT RESOLUTION FRAMEWORK

Sarah Asebedo (2016) published a Conflict Resolution Framework in the *Journal of Financial Therapy* that was developed from the conflict and mediation literature. The model is outlined in Figure 8.3 below.

Figure 8.3. Conflict Resolution Framework

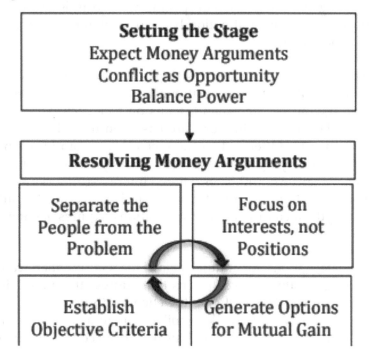

[A] Setting the Stage

It can be helpful to view conflict situations through the lens of Conflict Theory (see Chapter 7). Financial planners with an understanding of Conflict Theory will know that conflict is natural, and they should expect to encounter arguments and conflict around money. However, conflict also presents an opportunity. The conflict collaboration process can strengthen relationships and bring a deeper understanding of the other person and ourselves. Lastly, it is important to intentionally balance power when it comes to household finances because power imbalances in money matters can be detrimental to the household and create conflict. It is important to intentionally involve both partners in the financial planning process. Financial education can also be helpful where one client may be more detached from the finances due to feeling like they know less.

[B] Principles for Resolving Money Arguments

1. Separate the people from the problem: Identify the problem that is creating the conflict. Next, address the problem as a team. Avoid attacking or tearing down the person at all costs. Reframe any personal attacks and redirect attention back to resolving the problem that has been identified.

2. Focus on interests, not positions: Positions focus on *what* each person wants. Differing positions are typically the cause of conflicts. Interests, on the other hand, focus on *why* each person has taken a particular position. Interests are based on underlying values, needs, and concerns. Often, when the focus shifts from opposing positions to the underlying interests, commonality between the underlying interests can be found. These shared interests can serve as a foundation to collaborate to a conflict resolution. Discovering the interests and shifting the focus away from the positions requires openness, patience, and vulnerability.

3. Generate options for mutual gain: Financial planners can help their clients generate creative options that address the underlying interests in the conflict. This will give the clients a thorough understanding of their options as they work to collaborate to a conflict resolution. This will help to ensure that all options have been considered to see whether

necessary. It can be helpful to set a timeframe to make a decision so the conflict will not drag on indefinitely.

4. Establish objective criteria: The decision on how the conflict is to be resolved should be based on an objective criterion. As an impartial third party, financial planners can be particularly helpful in determining what this objective criterion should be.

8.7 STRATEGIES FOR MEDIATING A FINANCIAL CONFLICT

Brad Klontz, Neal Van Zutphen, and Kate Fries (2016) adapted 10 strategies to apply to handling conflict as a financial planner. Each of the 10 strategies you can use in practice are described below in Figure 8.4.

Figure 8.4. Ten Strategies a Financial Planner can Apply to Handle Conflict

Enhance skills in Psychology of Financial Planning	Seek out formal training and professional development in the Psychology of Financial Planning.
	Practice the skills described in this book with your colleagues and then with your clients.
	Consider earning a certificate or designation focused on Financial Coaching or Financial Therapy.
Focus on your role in the Psychology of Financial Planning planner-client relationship; identify your beliefs and biases that are inadvertently brought into client recommendations	Work through the introspective exercises laid out in this book.
	Make sure you have implemented your client recommendations in your own life and that you "practice what you preach."
Provide a comfortable physical space for clients to express cognitions and emotions openly	Don't play the news media on televisions in your office; this can increase clients' stress levels.
	Try to create less formal seating arrangements. Clients tend to be less comfortable when the table is between you and the client. Try to sit next to the client or sit in chairs without a table.
	If tables are a necessity, choose round and oval tables rather than rectangular or square tables.
Slow the process and reduce focus on immediate gratification in exchange for delayed gratification	Encourage face-to-face meetings on a regular basis. This creates dedicated time when the client can focus.
	Dedicate time and energy to developing an intentional financial planning process.
Create organization in a world of chaos	Consider setting data gathering meetings so clients are not overwhelmed during the intake process.
	If a client is consistently not taking action or seems overwhelmed, set an appointment to do the conference call together, download the statement together, etc.
	Take on the role of "financial quarterback" and help coordinate with other professionals (i.e., accountants, attorneys, etc.).
Be comfortable talking about the inevitability of death	Go through a "death rehearsal." Discuss details and differences in what would happen if your clients die simultaneously or at different times.
	Be persistent in discussing life insurance and estate planning recommendations and beneficiaries for avoidant clients. Discuss the implications for loved ones if the estate plan is not put in place.
Be overt in asking about anxiety	Help your clients pause, take a deep breath,and take a step back. Then reframe the situation, if possible.
	Help your clients examine the source or the trigger for the anxiety. Explore whether these sources can be reduced, avoided, or eliminated.
Be objective and straight-forward in observations and recommendations; do not sugarcoat reality	Be impartial.
	Overtly discuss any misalignment between a client's stated values/ goals and their behavior.
	Provide information, data, facts, and scenarios to provide clarity and a foundation to show what is known even in the midst of some uncertainty.
Normalize client's experiences	Create a safe, nonjudgemental space in your office to discuss money.
	Let clients know they are not alone in their experiences and that other people feel the same way they do.
	Use phrases like "it is ok to...", "it is common to...", etc. to normalize client experiences and feelings.
Make referrals and integrations with other professionals simple	Consider building a network of financial therapists and other mental health professionals. Start building your network and screening potential candidates

8.8 MEDIATING CONFLICT: DO'S AND DON'TS

The left-hand side of the chart below summarizes some of the key steps financial planners can take in mediating conflict. The column on the right contains steps that should be avoided as they can be detrimental in your pursuit of building a connection with your clients.

Do	Don't
• Do remain impartial in the face of a values conflict.	• Don't assume that conflict is always a bad thing.
• Do use the information in this chapter to identify when conflict is disrupting the financial planning process.	• Don't assume your role is to always fully resolve the conflict.
• Do work to understand your own preferred conflict style.	• Don't feel defeated if your are unable to help your clients resolve their conflict or if you encounter conflict yourself.
• Do seek to understand your clients' preferred conflict styles as you see them work through financial conflicts.	• Don't assume your clients will use the same conflict style every time. They may use different conflict styles in different situations.
• Do help your clients explore the reasons behind their conflict, especially if conflict is reoccuring frequently.	• Don't be a biased moderator in your client's financial conflict. Try to remain impartial.
• Do value the conflict process and understand the important outcomes of working through conflict in a healthy way.	
• Do establish a referral network for extreme conflicts (see Chapter 14).	

References

Asebedo, S. D. (2016). Building financial peace: A conflict resolution framework for money arguments. *Journal of Financial Therapy, 7*(2), 1-15.

Asebedo, S. and Purdon, E. (2018). Planning for conflict in client relationships. *Journal of Financial Planning, 31*(10), 48-56.

Britt, S. L., Hill, E. J., LeBaron, A., Lawson, D. R. and Bean, R. A. (2017). Tightwads and spenders: Predicting financial conflict in couple relationships. *Journal of Financial Planning, 30*(5), 36-42.

Collins Dictionary. (n.d.). Conflict. In *Collinsdictionary.com*. Retrieved March 2, 2023, from https://www.collinsdictionary.com/us/dictionary/english/conflict.

Klontz, B. T., Van Zutphen, N. and Fries, K. (2016). Financial planner as healer: Maximizing the role of financial health physician. *Journal of Financial Planning, 29*(12), 52-59.

Lutter, S. and Koochel, E. (2022). Mediating Financial Conflict. In S. Chatterjee, S. Lutter and D. Yeske (Eds.), *The Psychology of Financial Planning* (ch. 8). Certified Financial Planner Board of Standards, Inc.

National Endowment for Financial Education. (2018). Celebrate relationships, but beware of financial infidelity. https://www.nefe.org/news/2018/02/celebrate-relationships-but-beware-of-financial-infideltiy.aspx.

The Center for Nonviolent Communication. (n.d.). *NVC instruction self-guide*. CNVC.org. https://www.cnvc.org/online-learning/nvc-instruction-guide/nvc-instruction-guide.

Chapter 9

Facilitating Goal Congruence

9.1 INTRODUCTION

Goal incongruence occurs when couples have different goals for their lives or don't have specific goals that they are aiming for. Goal incongruence can be a challenge for financial planners and their coupled clients to overcome.

Goal incongruence should be expected. No two people are alike, so it is not surprising that people are likely to have different goals. Differences between people can lead to conflict, especially within a couple. Goal incongruence can cause financial conflict, and financial planners can serve in an important role as conflict mediators (discussed in more detail in Chapter 8). Financial planners can also serve their clients by helping them to manage their differences and move towards a common outcome and congruent goals.

9.2 FACILITATING GOAL CONGRUENCE IN PRACTICE

There are many opportunities for goal incongruence to become a factor in the financial planning process. Goal incongruence can occur based on fundamental differences in personal values. Goal incongruence can also occur based on specific circumstances that arise over the clients' lifetimes.

Goal incongruence can make it difficult for financial planners to implement the financial plan or even develop the financial plan. The second step in the financial planning process is identifying and selecting goals. If the goals cannot be identified for the client household, it is very difficult for the financial planning process to proceed.

The bullet points below list the most important takeaways for practitioners from Chapter 9: Facilitating Goal Congruence from the *Psychology of Financial Planning* (Kahler, 2022).

- Not all goal incongruence can be overcome. Close to 70% of things couples disagree about will not be overcome (Klontz et al., 2016). Sometimes managing goal incongruence is the best thing a financial planner can do.

- Financial planners can provide value to their clients when there is a disagreement about the couple's goals. The financial planner's role is to facilitate the process of moving from goal incongruence closer to goal congruence. During this process, the financial planner should remain impartial and unbiased.

- The financial planner should not avoid the conversation about goals if there is disagreement. The financial planner should also not set a compromise. If a compromise is necessary, it is important for the clients to come to a common understanding and identify an appropriate compromise themselves rather than having a "solution" imposed upon them. It is important for clients to engage in the process of discovering the values and feelings that drive their goals.

9.3 CLIENT AMBIVALENCE

Client ambivalence occurs when neither partner has a goal that they can work towards. If both clients are ambivalent, there are no goals to be achieved. Each may still be searching for the outcome they want to achieve, but they are certainly not on the same path to compatible goals.

In the case of client ambivalence, financial planners can help their clients move towards taking action and determining the goals for their financial plan. Chapter 6 contains a number of strategies to help clients work through goal ambivalence.

9.4 AVOIDING BIAS

When there is a disagreement between partners, it is essential to stay unbiased and not choose sides. This is also an essential skill when mediating a financial conflict (see Chapter 8). Below are some steps you can take to avoid exhibiting conscious (or unconscious) bias or favoritism.

- Spend fairly equal time speaking directly to both partners. If one partner is more talkative, be sure to engage the other partner in the conversation by asking them direct questions.

- Think of the client as the "couple" rather than thinking of the couple as two clients. When experiencing disagreements, advocate for the couple.

- Remain neutral even when one partner is "financially right" and the other partner is "financially wrong." Don't let one partner feel ganged up on.

- Drop your personal agenda. Listen with a "Beginner's Mind." Be open-minded and listen without making any pre-judgements.

9.5 TECHNIQUES FOR ADDRESSING GOAL INCONGRUENCE

[A] Normalize Incongruence

Explain to your clients that most clients are not in complete agreement about their goals. This may help your clients feel more comfortable with the incongruence and be able to approach the process of coming to a resolution more calmly and with a clearer head. You can normalize a client's feelings by using phrases like:

- It is understandable that you are feeling…

- It is okay to feel…

- That must have been a very [insert feeling adjective] experience.

- Your reaction is normal.

- A lot of people feel this way.

- You're not the only one going through this. A lot of other people experience what you are experiencing.

- This is a common problem/ experience. Other people have found [insert potential solution] to be helpful in situations like this.

[B] Curiosity

When clients are feeling "stuck," and don't know how to move forward to overcome goal incongruence, encourage your clients to practice curiosity. Curiosity is the desire to learn or know something. It is the opposite

Curiosity
The desire to learn or know something. The opposite of shaming and criticizing yourself.

of shaming or being critical of yourself. Talk to your clients about what curiosity is. Encourage them to be curious about why they feel a certain way, and to investigate why they are feeling internal conflict. Curiosity encourages an open mind. Curiosity may lead to a natural inclination to also investigate their partner's position with an open mind which may lead to a deeper understanding of what steps can be taken to bring more alignment within the couple. Curiosity can also increase intrinsic motivation which can help to overcome ambivalence.

Remember, different people have different innate levels of curiosity. Some of your clients may be more open to having a direct discussion about curiosity. With others, you may want to take a more indirect approach. Focus on your own curiosity about their situation and ask inquisitive and thoughtful questions to encourage the client to think more deeply about why they are feeling stuck.

Encouraging your clients to journal when they feel stuck can help them to foster a natural curiosity about their feelings, their thoughts, and their beliefs. It may be helpful to offer client specific journal prompts or even work together to develop journal prompts. A few journal prompts that could be adapted to various client situations are

Figure 9.1. Journal Prompts

What else might be going on in this situation? Why do we have different values when it comes to spending?

Why do I feel this way? Why do I want to prioritize current experiences over saving for the future?

Why is my partner so upset? Why does my partner feel angry when I increase my 401(k) salary deferral?

What could be possible if we find a solution to this incongruence? What could be possible if my partner and I can find a balance between current consumption and saving for our future goals?

What is most important in this situation? As my partner and I seek a solution to our different goals, what is important to me about the process of coming to a solution and what is important about the outcome?

[C] Separation of Behavior from Self

When there is incongruence between members of a couple, they can become frustrated with each other. In situations like this, it can be helpful to educate your clients about the concept of separation of behavior from self. If clients can separate their own behavior or their partner's behavior from their value as a person, this can encourage compassion and discourage shaming. This creates a much more productive environment to address the differences at play in the situation.

Money dialogue is an exercise that can help clients separate their self from their behavior. The steps for a money dialogue are as follows:

1. Ask the behavior why it does what it does.

2. Mentally switch places. Respond as the behavior to explain why.

3. As yourself, respond to the behavior.

4. Repeat until the dialogue comes to a natural conclusion.

The idea of a money dialogue can be difficult to conceptualize at first. See below for a script of a sample money dialogue addressing the financial behavior of saving.

Roberto: Why do you exist? How am I supposed to manage you, you fickle mistress? Saving is so difficult. Saving cash feels simple and doesn't feel overwhelming. But it is easier said than done, of course. Saving for investments feels like a monstrous, overwhelming task. How am I supposed to decide the best course of action for myself?

Money: You have to take time to research it on your own. If you still find it overwhelming or uncomfortable, then seek advice from someone who is more knowledgeable, a friend or a professional. But you need to have a foundation of financial knowledge so that you understand whether you agree with or accept the advice you receive.

Roberto: How much knowledge do I need? What level of detail do I need to go into? The problem with managing personal finances is that I was never educated about personal finances, so I don't know what my options are or how to determine what is even possible with my money.

Money: Do what you can. When you start to feel overwhelmed, you should start to seek help. Lots of people don't know how to manage their money, but acknowledging this will allow you to take the first step in feeling comfortable. Unfortunately, there is not one big answer that applies to everyone.

Roberto: I would like there to be just one answer. This does not make me feel better. But I understand why there is not one big answer like "if I do xyz, I'll be financially good." The only rule that comes to mind is don't spend more money than you have and go into debt as a consequence. But even doing that, you aren't necessarily going to get ahead financially.

Money: Relax a bit. You don't have to jump into saving and being perfect at managing your finances all at once. You are saving for a lifetime, so you don't need to rush. You are still young, and you have time to figure this out. Do you feel like you are struggling with saving right now?

Roberto: I feel like I'm managing, but when I start to feel comfortable with the amount I have, life seems to get in the way and sure enough a big expense comes out of nowhere. Which I realize is one of the reasons I should have savings, but it inhibits me from reaching my actual goal of living the life I want.

Money: Yeah, life tends to do that. You seem to have established two purposes for your savings, emergencies and trying to accomplish the life you want. These things you want to accomplish in life include your future retirement and fun stuff now, like vacations. Is there anything else?

Roberto: I feel behind in my savings goals, even though we are saving a really large proportion of our income. I want to buy a house but I'm also behind in my savings goals for retirement because I made a low income for most of my 20s. It feels like we will need to save for several more years to be able to buy a house if we keep our aggressive retirement savings on track. And I want to go back to school to increase my future income. I'm not sure how to prepare for all of this while trying to avoid a dull life.

Money: The truth is you are probably going to have to make some short-term sacrifices if you want to expedite this savings process. But that decision is completely up to you. The good thing about managing your personal finances is that ultimately you are the one who gets to make the decisions. You have brought up several valid points which shows you are at least actively thinking about this, and that is something to be proud of.

Roberto: Thanks. It seems like I might have a chance of making it to where I want to be.

This is a real money dialogue. There are some interesting things to note in this money dialogue. The process was very exhausting and challenging for "Roberto," and also for the financial planner. As a financial planner listening to a money dialogue, it is important to have minimal interjections, so that "Roberto" goes through this process himself. He should not feel like the financial planner is leading him in one direction or another, and he should not feel pressured to say what he feels he *should* say or what the financial planner is expecting

Several times during the process of speaking through the money dialogue exercise, Roberto got "stuck." He had to pause for several minutes to think and gather his thoughts. He felt like he could not continue with the exercise because he "didn't have the answers." When this happens, the financial planner should encourage Roberto to continue, reminding him to take his time and there is no rush. The financial planner should also acknowledge that the process is not easy. At the same time, the financial planner should be comfortable sitting in silence to allow Roberto to think without interjecting thoughts and encouragement constantly.

In this example, the financial planner recorded Roberto's verbal account of the money dialogue. If Roberto has engaged in this exercise alone and written down the dialogue himself, there are a few ways the financial planner could approach the follow-up after the exercise. Roberto may feel comfortable sharing what he wrote directly with the financial planner. However, even if Roberto does not want to share what he wrote, the financial planner can engage in a conversation with Roberto about what he learned during the exercise.

There are a few interesting things a financial planner can also learn about Roberto for the purposes of the financial planning process.

- Roberto does not feel confident in his knowledge of money.

- Roberto sees investing and saving as deeply connected. When speaking to "money," he initially spoke more about investing than saving. He also mentioned how stressful he finds investing specifically. This is a clue that Roberto may find conversations about investing deeply unpleasant and overwhelming. A financial planner should take care to separate saving from investing when discussing savings goals so that Roberto can feel more comfortable and confident going into the situation. Investing should be discussed intentionally, with Roberto clearly communicating how much investment education feels comfortable in any given meeting. Going into too much detail on investments all at once could cause more harm than good.

- Sometimes money makes Roberto feel helpless. A financial planner can provide value to Roberto by helping to build his confidence in his financial decisions by focusing on his strengths.

- Roberto seems to have a clear vision of what he wants his life to look like and how money can support this vision for his life. However, he did not go into detail during this exercise. As a follow-up to this exercise or as a next step, a financial planner could delve deeper into the conversation and ask Roberto open-ended questions and listen actively to how this vision for his life impacts his financial goals.

[D] Awareness of Emotions

Feelings can provide insight into the financial goal making process. Many of our financial goals are set subconsciously and based on our emotions. Clients aren't always immediately aware of their emotions, or they may struggle to articulate their feelings.

Mindfulness meditation has many benefits for both mental and physical health. Mindfulness meditation can help bring awareness to emotions and help to quiet the mind. Mindfulness meditation is helpful in relieving stress and anxiety as well as pain, depression, insomnia, and high blood pressure. For clients that are overwhelmed and anxious, mindfulness meditation can be very helpful bringing calm and awareness so that incongruence and conflict can be discussed with composure.

Clients may initially be resistant to trying mindfulness meditation. The National Center for Complementary and Integrative Health (2022) has compiled research about the health benefits of meditation and mindfulness. It can be helpful to educate your clients about the clinical trial results about the benefits of mindfulness meditation.

There is a plethora of resources available to learn how to guide people through mindfulness meditation and to learn how to practice mindfulness meditation. The basic steps are outlined in Figure 9.2. (Mindful.org, 2023).

Figure 9.2. Mindfulness Medication Steps

1. Find your seat.
- Choose a comfortable but solid seat where you can sit upright.
- A chair, meditation seat, or even a bench may be appropriate.

2. What are your legs doing?
- If you are sitting on the ground, cross your legs.
- If you are sitting in a chair, make sure the bottoms of your feet are fully touching the floor.

3. Straighten your upper body, but don't be stiff.
- Allow your spine to follow its natural curvature.

4. Position your arms parallel to your upper body.
- Place your hands on the top of your legs in a comfortable position.

5. Drop your chin. Allow your gaze to slowly descend.
- You may choose to close your eyes or just lower your eyelids.
- If you keep your eyes open, don't focus on any object in particular.

6. Be present in this position for a few moments.
- Make sure you are relaxed.
- Be aware of the sensations in your body.

7. Focus on your breath.
- Be aware of the act of breathing, the air coming in through your nose or mouth and then leaving your body. Feel the air coming in to your lungs and the rise of your chest.

8. Allow your attention to leave your breath and your thoughts to wander.
- It is completely normal for your mind to wander.
- Continue to focus on your breathing as thoughts are coming to you.
- Don't block any thoughts or try to clear your mind.

9. Don't make any physical movements without intention.
- Pause before you decide to move.

10. Allow your mind to continue to wander.
- Observe what you are thinking about without reacting.
- Don't be judgemental. Sit without any expectation.

11. When you're ready to end the meditation, open your eyes or slowly lift your gaze.
- Notice your environment.
- Notice how your body feels.
- Pause and decide how you intend to continue with your day.

9.6 FACILITATING GOAL CONGRUENCE: DO'S AND DON'TS

The left-hand side of the chart below summarizes some of the key steps financial planners can take to facilitate goal congruence. The column on the right contains steps that should be avoided as they can be detrimental in your pursuit of building a connection with your client.

Do	Don't
• Do consider using the Couples Money Listening Exercise described in Chapter 9 of the Psychology of Financial Planning with couples.	• Don't show or exhibit bias towards one partner or the other when there is disagreement or conflict related to goals (see Chapter 8 for a more in-depth discussion).
• Do use your listening skills to understand the underlying beliefs, values, and financial stories which are contributing to the incongruence.	• Don't have a personal agenda when meeting with clients.
• Do approach goal incongruence from a positive position, assuming the incongruence can be overcome. Ask your clients to describe a time they were able to overcome their differences.	• Don't jump right in and try to fix the problem or offer solutions right away.
• Help your clients move toward a place where they have a good understanding of their motivations, hopes, and fears and are able to express those feelings calmly and clearly.	• Don't feel you have failed if a perfect solution cannot be reached. It is more important to manage differences in a healthy way than to eliminate them.

Additional Resources

- Intimacy from the Inside Out™ (https://www.toniherbineblank.com/index.html)

- Internal Family Systems (https://ifs-institute.com/)

- Nonviolent Communication (see Chapter 8)

- Open-ended Questions (see Chapter 13)

- Mirroring (see Chapter 13)

- Active Listening (see Chapter 13)

- Transtheoretical Model of Behavior Change (see Chapter 2 and

- *Facilitating Financial Health: Tools for Financial Planners, Coaches, and Therapists* by Brad Klotz, Rick Kahler and Ted Klontz.

References

Kahler, R. (2022). Facilitating goal congruence. In S. Chatterjee, S. Lutter and D. Yeske (Eds.), *The Psychology of Financial Planning* (ch. 9). Certified Financial Planner Board of Standards, Inc.

Klontz, B., Kahler, R. and Klontz, T. (2016). *Facilitating Financial Health: Tools for Financial Planners, Coaches, and Therapists, 2nd Edition* (2nd ed.). The National Underwriter Company.

Mindful.org. (2023, January 6). *Mindfulness meditation: How to do it.* https://www.mindful.org/mindfulness-how-to-do-it/.

National Center for Complementary and Integrative Health. (2022, June). *Meditation and mindfulness: What you need to know.* National Institutes of Health. https://www.nccih.nih.gov/health/meditation-and-mindfulness-what-you-need-to-know.

Chapter 10

Identifying When Money is Being Used as Manipulation

10.1 INTRODUCTION

Money is a finite resource for every household. As such, it is natural that there may be competition over these resources and that money may be used to exert power. Manipulation is one way that this power struggle can be manifested. Financial manipulation

> **Financial Manipulation**
>
> Financial manipulation is using financial enabling, financial control, and financial abuse for personal gain.

can be defined as using financial enabling, financial control, and financial abuse for personal gain.

This chapter will help summarize the types of financial manipulation that planners may encounter in their practice. Best practices for financial planners will be provided in order to recognize elder abuse and guard against unintentionally manipulating your own clients. Please be aware, the topics in this chapter may be particularly difficult to read and think about.

10.2 FINANCIAL MANIPULATION IN PRACTICE

As a financial planner, you may witness instances of financial manipulation between clients in your practice. You may also encounter financial manipulation between your clients and their non-client family members. This can be particularly common in instances where a large inheritance is at play or clients are elderly or widowed. Their children may try to step in and manipulate their parents to ensure the financial outcome for themselves is optimal without a care to the financial well-being of their parent. In this instance, fiduciary financial planners have a duty to protect their clients.

The bulleted list below contains summarized highlights from Chapter 10: Identifying When Money is Being Used as Manipulation in *The Psychology of Financial Planning* (Davis et al., 2022).

- Financial manipulation can take the form of financial enabling, financial control, and financial abuse.

- Although financial planners are not trained to be equipped to handle and resolve these types of situations fully, there are certainly actions financial planners can take to facilitate better outcomes for clients, especially in situations where the financial manipulation is not intentional or malicious.

- In situations where financial abuse or dangerous manipulation are present, financial planners may consider making a referral to a mental health professional, family counselor, or other expert equipped with the skills to handle the situation appropriately.

- When encountering financial manipulation, financial planners can encourage egalitarian dynamics around money. Additionally, it can be helpful to work on increasing your clients' financial self-efficacy and the confidence of both partners. Encourage open and direct conversations around money.

10.3 TYPES OF FINANCIAL MANIPULATION AND ABUSE

Figure 10.1 outlines three different ways that financial manipulation can take place. Each manifestation of financial manipulation is defined

Figure 10.1. Financial Enabling, Control and Abuse

Financial Enabling

- What: An adult gives or lends money to a dependent adult knowing it will not be paid back.
- Why: Some people are uncomfortable saying no. Guilt or feeling responsible for something bad or uncomfortable that happened to the giftee. A desire to protect the giftee from financial stress or pain. Attempting to buy love, affection, or respect.
- Outcome: Damages the relationship between the enabler and the giftee. The enabler can feel resentment, depression, out of control, and experience decreased financial well-being. The receiver can feel incompetent, incapable, fear, anxiety, resentment, and decreased motivation for success.

Financial Control

- What: An imbalance of power in the financial decision-making of a family unit.
- Why: Differences in financial knowledge, income, and risk tolerance between members of the household.
- Outcome: Resentment and self-sabotage around financial goals.

Financial Abuse

- What: A type of abuse that involves experiencing financial fraud, having money or propery stolen, being put under financial pressure, and/or having financial assets or property misused.
- Why: Greed, entitlement, and a desire to control or harm.
- Outcome: Financial abuse and domestic violence are almost always present simultaneously.

10.4 FINANCIAL ABUSE SIGNALS

The National Network to End Domestic Violence [NNEDV] ("About Financial Abuse," n.d.) has compiled a list of ways financial abuse can happen. If you notice any of the events in the list in Figure 10.2 below happening to your clients, you should strongly consider how best you can help prevent the abuse from continuing.

Figure 10.2. Financial Abuse Events

• Forbidding the victim to work.

• Sabotaging work or employment opportunities by stalking or harassing the victim at the workplace or causing the victim to lose her/his job by physically battering prior to important meetings or interviews.

• Forbidding the victim from attending job training or advancement opportunities.

• Controlling how all of the money is spent.

• Not including the victim in investment or banking decisions.

• Not allowing the victim access to bank accounts.

• Withholding money or giving "an allowance."

• Forcing the victim to write bad checks or file fraudulent tax returns.

• Running up large amounts of debt on joint accounts.

• Refusing to work or contribute to the family income.

• Withholding funds for the victim or children to obtain basic needs such as food and medicine.

• Hiding assets.

• Stealing the victim's identity, property, or inheritance.

• Forcing the victim to work in a family business without pay.

• Refusing to pay bills and ruining the victims' credit score.

• Forcing the victim to turn over public benefits or threatening to turn the victim in for "cheating or misusing benefits."

• Filing false insurance claims.

• Refusing to pay or evading child support or manipulating the divorce process by drawing it out by hiding or not disclosing assets.

The NNEDV has also compiled a Financial Abuse Fact Sheet ("Financial Abuse Fact Sheet," n.d.) that contains information about financial abuse, the effects of financial abuse, and steps to take to rebuild from financial abuse. The fact sheet also contains additional resources for survivors of financial abuse.

10.5 ELDER ABUSE

As we age, we can become more mentally and physically vulnerable. Elder abuse is becoming an increasingly frequent occurrence, and it can take a variety of different forms. Physical abuse (e.g., hitting, kicking, etc.) is certainly one aspect of elder abuse, but elder abuse can also take the form of sexual abuse, emotional or psychological abuse, neglect and financial abuse. The CDC defines financial elder abuse as the "illegal, unauthorized, or improper use of an elder's money, benefits, belongings, property, or assets for the benefit of someone other than the older adult" (Centers for Disease Control and Prevention [CDC], 2021). Given financial planners knowledge of their client's financial assets and typical financial behaviors, financial planners may be able to identify instances of financial elder abuse if it is happening to their clients.

Figure 10.3 contains a list of the warning signs of elder abuse (National Institute on Aging, n.d.). Bear in mind, this list includes signs of all types of elder abuse, not just financial abuse. Financial planners should be aware of these signs as they communicate and meet with their elderly clients.

Figure 10.3. Warning Signs of Elder Abuse

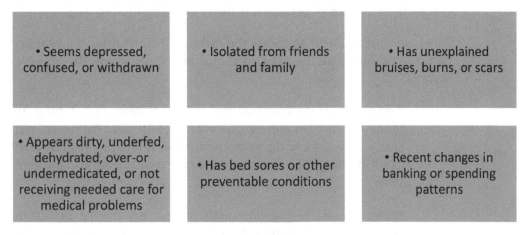

If you notice signs of elder abuse, you should contact your compliance department and document the situation thoroughly. It may be appropriate to contact the local Adult Protective Services, Long-Term Care Ombudsman, or the police.

10.6 BEWARE UNINTENDED MANIPULATION

It can be very easy for you as a financial planner to unintentionally manipulate your clients, especially if you have taken time to build own work understanding your financial history and financial trauma so that you can protect your clients from the unintended consequences of manipulating them into doing what you think is best even though what you think is best is not necessarily optimal for the client.

In psychotherapy, countertransference is said to occur when a therapist directs their emotions onto the client. These feelings can be problematic when there is a misalignment between how the therapist and the client feel about a situation. A similar issue can emerge in financial planning. There are several things you can do to protect your clients from countertransference. You can focus on the differences between yourself and your client so that you don't automatically assume their experiences are similar to your own. It may also make sense for you to work through deeper emotional and relational issues you've experienced with a therapist or counselor to ensure you work through those experiences in a healthy and productive way.

Meghaan Lurtz (2020) suggests the following steps financial planners can take to minimize the likelihood and impact of countertransference issues.

1. *Explore your subconscious beliefs about money* by taking the Money Script Inventory (Your Mental Wealth Advisors, n.d.) and/or by reviewing your own Money History (Lurtz, 2019) (see Chapter 5 for more information about how to take these steps).

2. *Review client relationships with a fresh perspective* by asking yourself the following questions and how the emotions in the questions below may have impacted your interactions and advice to clients:

   a. Are there current clients that make you feel angry?

   b. Are there current clients that make you feel stressed?

   c. Are there current clients that make you feel inadequate?

   d. Are there current clients that make you feel joy?

e. Are there current clients that make you feel excited?

f. Are there current clients that make you feel fulfilled?

3. *Reflect on how your personal money beliefs may be connected to your client relationships.* It may be helpful to journal or work with a financial therapist as you reflect intentionally about the connection between your client interactions and your money beliefs.

4. *Do a countertransference check-in with yourself after each client meeting* by asking yourself the following questions:

a. Am I stressed or happy?

b. What connections are being made in my mind about the client?

c. What did I learn from stopping and thinking about these connections?

d. After considering the answers to the questions above, how can I prepare for the next meeting or follow-up with that client?

5. *Do a countertransference check-in with yourself during a client meeting* if uncomfortable feelings are coming up for you:

a. How is your breathing? Are you breathing faster than usual? If so, why?

b. What are you feeling? Stress? Anger? Anxiety? Sadness? No matter what you are feeling, it is okay, and you can accept how you feel. Developing a deeper understanding of what we feel and why we feel what we feel can help us to react appropriately and thoughtfully.

6. *Consider working in teams when you meet with clients* as colleagues can be more objective and provide feedback. You will also be able to serve in the same capacity for your coworker during the meeting.

10.7 FINANCIAL MANIPULATION: DO'S AND DON'TS

The left-side column in the chart below summarizes how to identify and respond to financial manipulation. The column on the right contains steps that should be avoided as they can be detrimental in your pursuit of building a connection with your clients.

Do	Don't
• Do understand the resources available to your clients and yourself in an abusive or manipulative situation.	• Don't discount the impact your actions can have on others. You may unintentionally financially manipulate your family or your clients.
• Do learn to recognize the indicators of financial abuse and elder abuse.	• Don't ignore the warning signs of financial abuse.

Resource List

As part of the resources offered in this Practitioner's Resource Guide, the list below is a compilation of organizations and resources that are available to people who have experienced financial manipulation and abuse or the people who are working to help victims.

- Allstate Foundation's Relationship Abuse Program (https://allstatefoundation.org/what-we-do/end-domestic-violence/)

- Canadian Center for Women's Empowerment (https://ccfwe.org/what-is-economic-abuse/)

- Consumer Financial Protection Bureau (https://www.consumerfinance.gov/consumer-tools/educator-tools/resources-for-older-adults/reporting-elder-financial-abuse-guide/)

- Debt.org (https://www.debt.org/advice/financial-help-domestic-violence-victims/)

- Federal Trade Commission (*for taking back financial control of credit*) (https://www.ftc.gov/)

- Financial Crimes Enforcement Network (*when a crime has been committed*) (https://www.fincen.gov/)

- FINRA Foundation's *Taking Action: An Advocate's Guide to Assisting Victims of Financial Fraud* (https://www.finrafoundation.org/sites/finrafoundation/files/taking-action-an-advocates-guide-to-assisting-victims-of-financial-fraud_1.pdf)

- HelpGuide.org (https://www.helpguide.org/articles/abuse/getting-out-of-an-abusive-relationship.htm)

- MoneyGeek.com's *Finding Courage and Hope: Financial Support for Women Experiencing Domestic Violence* (https://www.moneygeek.com/financial-planning/resources/financial-help-women-abusive-relationships/)

- National Adult Protective Services Association (https://www.napsa-now.org/)

- National Institute on Aging (https://www.nia.nih.gov/health/elder-abuse)

- National Long-Term Care Resource Center (https://ltcombudsman.org/)

- National Network to End Domestic Violence (https://nnedv.org/)

- Office on Women's Health (https://www.womenshealth.gov/relationships-and-safety)

- WomensLaw.org (https://www.womenslaw.org/laws)

References

Centers for Disease Control and Prevention. (2021, June 2). *Fast facts: Preventing elder abuse.* https://www.cdc.gov/violenceprevention/elderabuse/fastfact.html.

Davis, S., Lurtz, M. and McCoy, M. (2022). Identifying when money is being used as manipulation. In S. Chatterjee, S. Lutter and D. Yeske (Eds.), *The Psychology of Financial Planning* (ch. 10). Certified Financial Planner Board of Standards, Inc.

Lurtz, M. (2019, June 5). Finding your own money story to better communicate with clients. *Kitces.com.* https://www.kitces.com/blog/margaret-atwood-payback-debt-book-money-script-egg-narrative/.

Lurtz, M. (2020, September 23). Fostering healthier advisor-client relationships by mitigating transference and counter-transference. *Kitces.com.* https://www.kitces.com/blog/transference-counter-transference-client-advisor-relationship-projection-money-scripts/.

National Institute on Aging. (n.d.). *Spotting the signs of elder abuse.* National Institutes of Health. https://www.nia.nih.gov/health/infographics/spotting-signs-elder-abuse.

National Network to End Domestic Violence. (n.d.). *About financial abuse.* NNEDV.org. https://nnedv.org/content/about-financial-abuse/.

National Network to End Domestic Violence. (n.d.). *Financial abuse fact sheet.* NNEDV.org. https://nnedv.org/resources-library/financial-abuse-fact-sheet/.

Your Mental Wealth Advisors. (n.d.). *Your money script.* https://www.yourmentalwealthadvisors.com/our-process/your-money-script/.

Chapter 11

Applying Financial Counseling Skills to the Financial Planning Process

11.1 INTRODUCTION

You do not need to be a financial counselor to benefit from the resources and techniques described in this chapter. Financial counselors "help provide educational and emotional support and guidance to their clients that helps them to confidently take effective action on their personal financial matters" (National Financial Educators Council, n.d.). Financial counselors take a different approach and play a different role than most financial planners. Financial counselors often focus on topics such as debt management, credit management, budgets, mortgages, bankruptcy, retirement planning, estate planning, and taxes. While financial planners typically take over as much of the financial management as possible on behalf of the client, financial counselors typically focus on educating the client and/or partnering with the client to accomplish their goals. Financial counselors are typically paid hourly; the financial planning AUM model does not work in financial counseling as financial counselors do not manage assets or investment portfolios on behalf of their clients.

In addressing a client's overall financial wellness, financial counselors are trained to encourage financial transparency, establish trusting relationships, recognize signs of resistance, and use communication and listening skills. Financial planners and their clients can benefit greatly from incorporating these skills in the financial planning process as well. If possible, financial planners should consider seeking formal training in these areas as these skills can be used daily in client work. Financial planners can turn to these core tenets of counseling theory to improve their interpersonal skills and develop deeper, richer relationships with clients, building a strong foundation upon which to work towards the client's goals.

11.2 FINANCIAL COUNSELING SKILLS IN PRACTICE

Most financial planners are already using financial counseling skills to some degree in their work with clients. Although you may already be incorporating some or all of these skills in your practice, be patient with yourself as you work to intentionally develop these skills further. Additionally, seek feedback from colleagues as they may be able to help you understand which skills you are already strong in and which skills you may want to focus on advancing further.

The arrows below summarize the most important concepts for financial planning practitioners from Chapter 11: Applying Financial Counseling Skills to the Financial Planning Process in *The Psychology of Financial Planning* (Koochel et al., 2022).

- Transparency, establishing trust, communication, and cultural humility are some of the most important financial counselling skills for financial planners to develop.

- Financial planners deal with sensitive and highly personal information. It is normal for clients to feel resistant or apprehensive to being fully transparent about their finances, particularly early in the planning relationship.

- Communication occurs verbally and nonverbally, both in-person and virtually.

- Developing a trusting relationship with the client is an important first step in helping motivate clients to take action or change behavior.

11.3 TRANSPARENCY

Time and experience will alert you to something not adding up. Make sure that the client understands that you are not here to judge. "Is there anything else" is a great question in this situation and it may be helpful in getting them to tell you more about their history. Transparency goes both ways. Be sure to allow the client to ask you questions – "Is there anything that you would like to ask me?"

11.4 ESTABLISH A TRUSTING RELATIONSHIP

Take the time at the beginning of the relationship to understand what is most important and why. Spend more time listening than talking. When working with a couple, make sure that you are hearing from both parties. Build the relationship by conversing about family, blessings and hardships. Show empathy. Do not say that you know how they feel – you can't possibly know. But you can understand that something was stressful, terrible, exciting, or once in a lifetime.

Resistance – If things are going too well, something likely is wrong. Some resistance is normal and is an opportunity for clarification or to learn something about the client that has not been previously presented. Resistance is often a reaction to having been talking "at" clients, rather than talking "to" them. They may fear being judged for their lack of understanding about a topic or strategy.

11.5 COMMUNICATION SKILLS

Eye contact is vital to a trusting relationship. Sometime this can be difficult. If a prospect cannot look you in the eye, be wary. It may take longer to develop a trusting relationship.

You may have the opportunity to work with someone who has a disfigurement or a tic or something that makes it difficult for you to have eye contact. Maybe you feel like you are staring and making them uncomfortable. Look for an opportunity to ask about it. Usually, this clears the air, and you both become more comfortable.

Be comfortable but be "quiet." Avoid excessive body movements.

We don't often have the luxury of having formal and informal seating in our meeting space. The popularity of Zoom has allowed us the luxury of meeting people where they are most comfortable, and for this reason, Zoom has been a facilitator for many deeper conversations. Virtual meetings are the norm for many firms' advisors. It is always best to ensure the client and the advisor are in private locations and where disruptions will be minimized. Although this is very important, this can be difficult with children in the home or colleagues in the office.

Remember, the desk or conference table is a barrier – this can be good or bad depending on the client. But one thing is very irksome – be sure that your chair height is not higher than the client's chair height.

Speak at reasonable pace. Do not rush and do not rush the client. Give the client time to process what you have said. Some silence is good, but how long should you wait? If it seems too long, you might ask – "Do you want me to elaborate on that?" Sometimes when working with a couple, one will need some space to process something the other said. When you start to see signs of disagreement between a couple, it is important to be sure that you hear both.

We are not therapists, so know when you are in over your head. In this situation, you can use phrases and questions like: "You seem to have a lot of reasons why this is going to be difficult for you. Do you have anyone else to talk to about why this seems hard?"

Listen – this is the best opportunity you have to learn more about what is most important to your client. Ask questions that are particular to what the client just told you to gain a deeper understanding. For example: "That must have been very special. How did you celebrate?" or "That must have been a very difficult time. How did you get through it?"

11.6 UNDERSTANDING AND DEVELOPING GOALS

Some people have a difficult time defining and articulating their financial goals. Regardless of their stage in life, it is helpful to understand what is important to the client and the context of why it matters. This is especially important in the case where a goal may be unreasonable or difficult to reach due to time and circumstances. Getting the client to tell a personal story about why funding a college education for children, or grandchildren, is a primary goal, for example, will provide context for the financial planner to recommend acceptable alternative recommendations when that goal cannot be entirely met.

Helping the client to be more specific about goals and understanding context can help in ranking the relative importance of goals and alignment with client values. This process helps to develop deeper relationships, aids the financial planner in framing recommendations, and can lead to better client acceptance and implementation especially in difficult circumstances.

11.7 NONVERBAL CUES LIST

Figure 11.1 contains a list of nonverbal cues that may give insight into how a client may truly be feeling. The nonverbal cues are listed in the darker boxes. Below each box, the bullet points summarize the emotions the nonverbal cue may be pointing to.

Figure 11.1. Nonverbal Cues

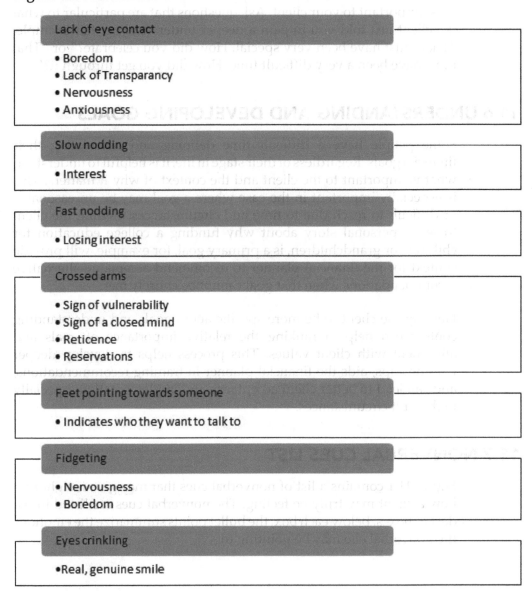

11.8 CULTURAL HUMILITY

Cultural humility is an essential component of counseling theory. Before beginning to understand the identities of your colleagues or your clients, you should work to understand your own cultural identity. In Figure 11.2 in the empty box or the open space next to each letter of the ADDRESSING mnemonic device, write in your own words how you identify for each of these ten dimensions of identity.

Figure 11.2. ADDRESSING Mnemonic Device for the Ten Dimensions of Identity

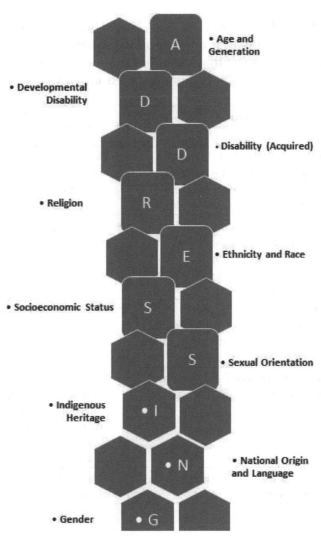

Once you have identified your own cultural identity, work to understand the historical realities of oppression and structural racism and expand your cultural knowledge to develop your cultural awareness (Koochel, 2022). Culturally competent financial planners may be able to build deeper, more trusting, and more authentic relationships with their clients.

11.9 FINANCIAL COUNSELING SKILLS: DO'S AND DON'TS

The left-side column in the chart below summarizes financial counseling skills that are important to develop. The column on the right contains steps that should be avoided as they can be detrimental in your pursuit of building a connection with your clients.

Do	Don't
• Do understand that financial transparency may be more difficult for some clients than others.	• Don't assume the client was completely transparent with you just because the meeting felt like it went well.
• Do know a lack of financial transparency may be rooted more in discomfort about talking about money than a desire to be willfully deceptive.	• Don't assume all nondisclosure is intentional.
• Do ask the client "is there anything else?" to prompt clients to think whether any information is missing unintentionally.	• Don't stop your client from formulating their own solutions.
• Do create a space for clients to share their financial worries.	• Don't see resistance as a failure of the client or the planner nor should it be viewed as stubbornness or noncompliance. Resistance is feedback for the planner.
• Do normalize your client's experiences.	• Don't mirror every movement the client makes.

• Do use effective communication, active listening, and cultural awareness to build a trusting relationship with the client.	• Don't use closed-ended questions if you can use an open-ended question instead.
• Do show optimism and focus on positive outcomes of change when you encounter resistance.	• Don't let your persistent inner dialogue prevent you from truly listening to what your client is communicating to you.
• Do use reflective listening and reflective responses when you encounter resistance.	• Don't be judgemental.
• Do use eye contact and leaning forward to convey the client has your full attention.	• Don't stereotype. Strive for cultural humility.
• Do use basic pacing techniques like restating, reflecting, and summarizing.	
• Do be mindful of how your meeting space is laid out and the color palette you choose for your office.	
• Do expand your cultural knowledge.	

References

Koochel, E. (2022, May 26). *3 Financial counseling skills for financial planners*. eMoney. https://emoneyadvisor.com/blog/3-financial-counseling-skills-for-financial-planners/.

Koochel, E., McCoy, M. and Davis, S. (2022). Applying financial counseling skills to the financial planning process. In S. Chatterjee, S. Lutter and D. Yeske (Eds.), *The Psychology of Financial Planning* (ch. 11). Certified Financial Planner Board of Standards, Inc.

National Financial Educators Council. (n.d.). *What is a financial counselor*. https://www.financialeducatorscouncil.org/what-is-a-financial-counselor/.

Chapter 12

Forging Trusting Relationships

12.1 INTRODUCTION

Trust in an important part of every long-term financial planner-client relationship. Trust impacts the quality of the planning relationship. The quality of the planning relationship impacts the longevity of the relationship and can also impact the client's willingness to take action.

> **Trust**
>
> Trust is made up of two components: credibility trust and benevolence trust. Credibility trust is trust in the advisor's technical competence. Benevolence trust is confidence that the financial planner will act in the client's best interest.

Trust can be conceptualized in a number of different ways. For the purposes of this chapter, the definition of trust is based on trust having multiple components: credibility trust and benevolence trust (Sharpe et al., 2007). Credibility trust is trust in the advisor's technical competence. Benevolence trust is confidence that the financial planner will act in the client's best interest.

This chapter will lay a foundation for the importance of trust in the financial planner-client relationship. Additionally, it will provide practical steps you can take to build trust with your clients as well as

12.2 FORGING TRUSTING RELATIONSHIPS IN PRACTICE

It can take time for trust to be built between financial planners and their clients. If you earn a client's trust, you should appreciate this trust. Trust can translate to client referrals as well as longevity in client relationships.

As a baseline for earning and maintaining trust, it is important to meet the client's needs. Make sure you are returning phone calls and emails in a timely manner. Clients should feel like they are important to you and that you have time to give them personal attention. Listen actively to your clients and be consistent in your behavior towards them. Remember, trust building may begin even before a prospect has contacted you. And above all, act ethically and with integrity in accordance with the fiduciary standard.

The following list contains valuable takeaways for financial planning practitioners from Chapter 12: Forging Trusting Relationships in *The Psychology of Financial Planning* (McCoy and Lutter, 2022).

- Once a financial planner has earned a client's trust, it is important to behave consistently otherwise you may break the client's trust. Trust, once broken, is very difficult to repair and can be quite fragile. Sometimes, trust is impossible to repair.

- Trust can lead to better outcomes for the client if you are truly making recommendations that are in the client's best interests. Clients that trust their financial advisor are more likely to implement recommendations.

- Most financial planners overestimate how much their clients trust them.

- Clients' past experiences may impact how easy or difficult it is for them to trust their financial planner.

- Client-oriented planning practices are typically more effective at building trust with clients than sales-oriented practices.

12.3 COMPONENTS OF TRUST

A Vanguard study conceptualized trust as having three different components: functional factors, emotional factors, and ethical factors (Madamba and Utkus, 2017) (see Figure 12.1). Each of these components have a different level of impact on overall trust. The study found that the emotional components of trust make up about 53% of overall trust, the ethical components of trust make up about 30% of overall trust, and the functional components of trust make up about 17% of overall trust. Although all components listed here are important for building a trusting relationship with a client, it is interesting that the emotional components are more important than the ethical and the functional components combined.

The emotional components of trust include the intangible aspects of the client-planner relationship that can bring about positive feelings. These factors include making the client feel like their goals are important, the client feeling like the financial planner relates to the client, the client feeling they can sleep well at night, the client not feeling rushed, and the client feeling like the planner can view the world from the client's perspective.

The ethical components of trust include the financial planner always acting in accordance with the client's best interests, acting with integrity and morality, avoiding conflicts of interest, being compensated reasonably, and being willing to admit if they don't know the answer to the client's question.

The functional components of trust include knowing how to create, execute, and reassess the financial plan and being proactive in contacting the clients regarding their investment portfolios. Other functional components include the financial planner doing what they said they would do, the financial planner having relevant industry qualifications, the financial planner being aware of trends in the financial markets, the financial planner being able to make planning suggestions on the spot, and the financial advisor being well connected in the community.

Figure 12.1. Components of Trust

Functional (17%)	Emotional (53%)	Ethical (30%)
• Financial industry qualifications • Creation and execution of financial plan • Proactive communications	• Intangible aspects of the relationship between the client and planner that bring about positive feelings • "My advisor is my advocate" (17%) • "My advisor provides a sense of relief" • "My advisor makes me feel my portfolio is important" • "My advisor is someone I can relate to or make a connection with"	• Absence of conflicts of interest • Charging reasonable fees • Acting in the best interests of the client (15%)

12.4 EARNING TRUST

Understanding the factors that impact a client's trust in a financial planner is an important first step in building a trusting relationship. The next step involves taking actions that will earn trust with a client. Research has shown that there are five core beliefs that can help drive trust in a financial planner (Swift and Littlechild, 2015):

- My advisor takes the time to understand my financial needs and concerns.

- My advisor fully understands my goals for the future.

- My advisor gives me peace of mind.

- My advisor clearly explains difficult financial concepts.

- When making recommendations regarding our plan or our portfolio, my advisor puts the needs of me and my family first.

Other research studies have broken down the actions that financial planners can take to build trust with their clients even further. Figure 12.2 below breaks down the concept of trust building into four different categories and includes the steps financial planners can take to build trust with their clients.

Figure 12.2. Four Categories of Trust Building

Ethical Behavior
- Operate with integrity and objectivity.
- Display an ethical work culture across the whole team.
- Provide clients and employees with a physical copy of a code of ethics.
- Include ethics or ethical behavior in your company's mission statement.

Pricing and Quality of Products and Services Offered
- Recommendations must align with the client's needs.
- Clearly describe how recommendations relate to the financial plan.
- Price your services fairly.

Compensation Arrangements
- Institutionalize transparency about how the financial planner will be paid.
- Offer information proactively.

Marketing and Client Experiences
- Make sure the factors that build trust are built into your brand and the client experience.
- Create an excellent financial plan.
- Put efficient client operation procedures in place.
- Implement high quality communication standards.
- Make your clients feel valued, respected, and understood.

12.5 PRACTITIONER TAKEAWAYS FROM COMMITMENT-TRUST THEORY

Commitment-Trust Theory provides a helpful theoretical framework for practitioners to understand the different factors that impact commitment and trust (Morgan and Hunt, 1994). Understanding the system through which trust is built theoretically can help financial planners to determine which factors are within their control and what steps can be taken to leverage these factors (see Figure 12.3).

Figure 12.3. Commitment-Trust Theory – Factors that Impact Commitment and Trust

Factor	Know	Implement
Relationship Termination Costs	The higher the relationship termination costs (i.e., time, energy, and money needed to find a new financial planner), the more committed the financial planner-client relationship will be.	Communicate frequently with both partners in the client household and involve children in the financial planning process.
Relationship Benefit	The higher the perceived benefit of the client-planner relationship, the more committed the client will be to the relationship.	Financial planners should focus on communicating and demonstrating their value.
Opportunistic Behavior	Opportunistic behavior, actions that are clearly motivated by self-interest potential loss to the client, will decrease the client's trust in the financial planner.	Uphold the fiduciary standard, and truthfully communicate how your recommendations are in the client's best interests. Communicate your fee structure clearly and openly. Avoid all types of opportunistic behavior.
Communication	Communication is a big precursor to trust. Communication builds trust, and trust can improve and facilitate communication. Trust allows the client to assume the financial planner has good intentions in communication, and financial planners can communicate more directly with clients.	Communicate skillfully and intentionally. Use verbal communication, nonverbal communication, and spatial arrangement in your meeting environment to your advantage. Chapter 13 contains more details about communication best practices.
Shared Values	Shared values between the client and the planner must be in place for relationship commitment and trust to develop.	Be open with your clients about your values. Do the introspective work of understanding your values, so that you can communicate authentically with

By implementing the suggestions in the Implement column, financial planners can expect to build a client's commitment and trust. Through building a client's commitment, clients will be more receptive to advice, will be more likely to continue working with you, and will be more cooperative. By building trust, it will be easier to resolve disagreement with clients, clients will be more decisive, confident, and cooperative. See Figure 12.4 below.

Figure 12.4. Building a Client's Commitment to Generate Trust

12.6 ADDITIONAL OUTCOMES OF BUILDING TRUST

Closer cooperation, easier disagreement resolution, and increased client confidence are not the only outcomes associated with high levels of client trust. Clients with high levels of trust are more likely to refer people to their financial planner (Swift and Littlechild, 2015), and referrals are an important source of business for financial planners (Madamba and Utkus, 2017). The same study found that clients are also more willing to invest additional funds with a financial advisor if they have a high level of trust in the advisor. Not surprisingly, clients that trust their advisor are less likely to leave the financial planner, so

12.7 BREAKING TRUST

The same Vanguard study cited previously found that the two most common instances of breaking trust in a client-planner relationship involve investment performance and neglecting the relationship (Madamba and Utkus, 2017). In that study, about 22% of the respondents had had their trust broken by a financial advisor. The ways in which their trust was broken are listed in Figure 12.5 in descending order from the most frequent way that trust was broken to the least frequent way trust was broken.

Figure 12.5. Breaking Trust in a Client-Planner Relationship

%	Reason
46%	Caused my portfolio to underperform
44%	Did not pay enough attention to me or my portfolio
43%	Steered me toward poor investment choices given my risk tolerance and goals
35%	Did not achieve what they set out to achieve for me
34%	Did not make me feel that my business or portfolio was important
34%	Lack of timely communication
25%	Did not follow up or do what they said they would do
22%	Condescending
21%	Did not explain things to me in a way I understood
20%	Did not take my concerns or questions seriously
19%	Did not understand me as an investor
18%	Did not act morally
6%	Did not respect my spouse as an equal partner
5%	Took advantage or acted in own interest
4%	Poor advice or investment decisions
3%	Acted illegally
2%	

Perceived breakage of trust by underperforming a client's expectations regarding their investment performance is a particularly interesting reason for trust to be broken. Financial planners may feel this is an "unfair" reason for trust to be broken given that market performance, a largely uncontrollable factor, is a large factor in overall client return. Financial planners can be proactive in addressing the potential for this factor to impact their client relationships by educating prospects about reasonable return expectations rather than setting themselves up to overpromise and underperform. It is essential to set realistic expectations from the start of the client-planner relationship.

12.8 REPAIRING BROKEN TRUST

Trust can be broken intentionally and unintentionally. Mistakes can happen, but sometimes when trust is broken, trust is lost forever. For this reason, client trust should be treasured, and it should not be taken lightly. As illustrated in Figure 12.6, the University of Minnesota Extension suggest the following process for working to repair trust once it has been broken (Rasmussen, 2021).

Figure 12.6. Process to Repair Trust

1. Acknowledge and own your part in what happened.
- Without acknowledging what you did was wrong, no client has a reason to trust you again.

2. Allow negative feelings to surface.
- Give the client space to express how they feel: anger, disapointment, sadness, etc. Listen to what they have to say, and acknowledge the validity of their feelings.
- Give yourself space to process your own feelings.

3. Make a commitment to a new behavior.
- Start small with rebuilding the client's trust to make sure you can be consistent.
- Explain to the client how you will be doing things differently going forward.

4. Allow time for temporary unsettledness and new behavior.
- It will take some clients longer to be able to let go of the past than others. The amount of time it takes may also depend on the severity of the situation. In either case, expect this step to take a significant amount of time.

5. Go back to step 3 or let go and move on.
- If you are able to repair the trust, you can move forward with the client and hopefully have a long and happy planning relationship.

12.9 FORGING TRUSTING RELATIONSHIPS: DO'S AND DON'TS

The left-side column in the chart below summarizes how to forge trusting relationships with clients. The column on the right contains steps that should be avoided as they can be detrimental in your pursuit of building a connection with your clients.

Do	Don't
• Do treasure the trust you build with your clients. It should not be taken lightly.	• Don't tell your clients' secrets. Maintain confidentiality.
• Do keep promised due dates and deadlines.	• Don't overpromise.
• Do provide appropriate communication to your clients to avoid perceived differences in what a client thinks you can deliver and control and what you can actually deliver and control.	• Don't daydream or appear distracted when interacting with a client. Show the client that they are important to you.
• Do maintain eye contact with a client during in-person meetings and virtual meetings.	• Don't check devices during in-person or virtual meetings.
• Do regularly check-in with clients using the communication techniques described in Chapter 13.	• Don't be too directive with the client, especially in the beginning of the planning relationship.
• Do ask for clarification from a client	• Don't brush clients off, ignore their questions, or diminish their concerns, especially clients who are grieving a recent loss. Your client needs to feel understood, and you need to learn about their concerns and priorities.
• Do be genuinely curious about the client and their family.	• Don't use jargon, if possible. Use plain, clear language that the client can understand.

• Do develop cultural competency (see Chapter 11) to facilitate trust building.	• Don't avoid conversations about repairing trust if you have broken a client's trust. It is your responsibility to initiate the conversation nondefensively while being open and direct.
• Do be present in meetings.	
• Do create a welcoming office environment.	
• Do a pre-mortem analysis rather than a post-mortem analysis on your valued relationships. Imagine it is one year in the future and that relationship has failed. Considering what failure looks like can help you to avoid mistakes.	
• Do ask your clients "what would you like to accomplish today" or "how will we know we have had a successful meeting today" at the start of a meeting.	
• Do end your meetings by asking "is there anything else?" It is ok to ask this multiple times if there are multiple things that the client still wants to discuss. This will allow the client an opportunity to share anything else that is on their mind.	
• Do connect your recommendations directly and demonstrably to the client's personal values and goals.	
• Do anything and everything to make the client feel truly heard and understood.	

References

Madamba, A. and Utkus, S. (2017). *Trust and financial advice* [White paper]. Vanguard. https://static.vgcontent.info/crp/intl/gas/canada/documents/trust-and-advice-research.pdf.

McCoy, M. and Lutter, S. (2022). Forging trusting relationships. In S. Chatterjee, S. Lutter and D. Yeske (Eds.), *The Psychology of Financial Planning* (ch. 12). Certified Financial Planner Board of Standards, Inc.

Morgan, R. M. and Hunt, S. D. (1994). The commitment-trust theory of relationship marketing. *Journal of Marketing, 58*(3), 20-38.

Rasmussen, C. (2021, September 27). *Five steps for rebuilding trust*. University of Minnesota Extension. https://extension.umn.edu/community-news-and-insights/five-steps-rebuilding-trust.

Sharpe, D. L., Anderson, C., White, A., Galvan, S. and Siesta, M. (2007). Specific elements of communication that affect trust and commitment in the financial planning process. *Journal of Financial Counseling and Planning, 18*(1), 2-17.

Swift, M. and Littlechild, J. (2015). Building trust through communication. *Journal of Financial Planning, 28*(11), 28-32.

Chapter 13

Multifaceted Communication

13.1 INTRODUCTION

Communication is the process of interacting through messages (Gerbner, 1958). These messages can be verbal and nonverbal. They can be obvious or subtle. They can be intentionally or unintentionally communicated. These messages are constantly communicated between

> **Communication**
>
> The process of interacting through messages. The process of sharing information that can foster mutual understanding in a client-planner relationship.

financial planners and their clients. Communication in financial planning is often used with the intent of fostering a mutual understanding between the financial planner and the client (Grable and Goetz, 2017).

Communication skills and the importance of strong communication with clients has been touched on in every chapter of this book. Investing time in developing strong communication skills and learning new communication techniques will benefit you in every aspect of the psychology of financial planning, from expressing authentic empathy to gathering data about your client's goals, values, and risk tolerance.

Every financial planner uses communication skills on a daily basis. Communication skills may be something you know you need to work on, or you may already be an excellent communicator. Regardless of your overall skill level in communication, this chapter will provide you with steps and processes for using a variety of communication techniques. Some of these techniques may not feel natural at first and some may never feel natural. You may have to invest significant time to develop your comfort and skill level with using them. Start by trying out these communication skills in your everyday life before you try to use them with clients. Some people have inherent talent when it comes to communicating, but typically communication skills are more likely to be learned and refined through study and practice.

In addition to the resources laid out in this chapter and in the *Psychology of Financial Planning*, the CFP Board *Communication Essentials for Financial Planners: Strategies and Techniques* offers many resources for financial planners wanting to enhance their communication skills.

13.2 MULTIFACETED COMMUNICATION IN PRACTICE

Although strong communication skills are required at every step of the financial planning process, few financial planners receive formal training in communication skills. Communication has the power to build a strong relationship between the financial planner and the client which can serve as a foundation for the entire planning engagement and planning process. Financial planners use verbal communication to gather the necessary data to formulate recommendations. However, nonverbal communication is just as important to the planning process. Financial planners can obtain clues about their clients' feelings related to the recommendations through the clients' nonverbal cues like tone and body language. Clients' nonverbal cues can communicate stress, joy, confusion, etc. which are important for planners to understand so that they can respond appropriately to the client.

Below are a few key takeaways from Chapter 13: Multifaceted Communication in the *Psychology of Financial Planning* (Chatterjee and Sages, 2022).

- Communication is typically used to build trust, to share information, and to facilitate financial decision-making

- Although communication can be categorized into four types (i.e., interpersonal, intrapersonal, group, and mass communication), financial planning primarily involves interpersonal communication. Interpersonal communication techniques are the primary focus of this chapter.

> **Types of Communication**
>
> **Interpersonal Communication** – Communication between two people or a small group of people.
>
> **Intrapersonal Communication** – Communication with yourself.
>
> **Group Communication** – Communication to large groups of people.
>
> **Mass Communication** – Communication to very large groups (i.e., the masses).

- Ineffective communication skills can hurt a client's perception of your level of knowledge and competence.

- Pay attention to the environment when you are communicating with clients as this can have an effect on the communication process. For example, if the room is noisy or too hot or too cold, this can create significant distractions which inhibit effective communication.

13.3 VERBAL COMMUNICATION

When thinking about communication skills, verbal communication, the words we say and how we say them, are typically the first thing that comes to mind. Verbal communication skills are essential for accurately conveying meaning between the financial planner and the client. Verbal communication skills include verbal pacing, restating, paraphrasing, and summarizing (these techniques are discussed later in the chapter).

Appreciative Inquiry

Appreciative inquiry involves asking positively framed questions and queries. Appreciative inquiry requires a positive perspective to value people and their strengths, possibilities, and successes (Coghlan et al., 2003). In applying appreciative inquiry to financial planning, financial planners can ask questions and queries like:

- What do you like about the decision to reallocate your

- What has been good about your previous work with financial professionals?

- Do you have a particular positive memory around money from your childhood?

- What are the best aspects of how you have been managing your money thus far?

- What strengths have you and your partner been using to manage your money? How can you continue leveraging those strengths to continue working towards your financial goals?

- Describe a time when you used one of your strengths to meet a financial goal.

- Describe a time when you were successful in increasing your savings rate.

13.4 QUESTIONING CLIENTS

There is more than one way to ask a question. You may not often think intentionally about how you are structuring or formulating your questions. The different types of questions you can ask and examples of how they can be formulated are in Figure 13.1. You should be thoughtful in how you formulate your questions. You may wish to pause slightly before asking an important question to consider how best to structure the question. As you gain more experience formulating thoughtful questions and experimenting with question structures, you will start to feel more comfortable with using varied questions structures. Skillful questions can help you gather richer information from your clients and develop deeper relationships with them.

Figure 13.1. Types of Client Questions

Open-Ended Questions

- Cannot be answered with a simple "yes" or "no" answer.
- Usually begins with what, who, when, why, how, or tell me.
- Example: How did you decide on your previous portfolio allocation?

Closed-Ended Questions

- Can typically be answered with a simple "yes" or "no."
- Usually begins with "are you...", "do you...", "is this...", or "is that...".
- Example: Did you previously invest your 401(k)?

Question Transformation

- The question is initially structured as an open-ended question, but a phrase is added at the end to make the question closed-ended.
- This question type typically does not serve a useful function, and should be avoided. It can also make the client feel like you are leading them to answer a certain way.
- Example: What estate planning preparations have you made - do you even have a will?

Swing Question

- Structured like a closed-ended question, but it usually doesn't lead a client to just answer "yes" or "no."
- Usually begins with "will," "can," "could," or "would."
- Example: Could you tell me whether you have contacted a real estate agent to sell your home?

Implied or Indirect Questions

- Should only be used once you have a well established relationship with the client.
- Usually begins with "I wonder" or "you must."
- Example: You must be planning a trip sometime soon.

Projective Questions

- Can be used to solicit unconscious thoughts, values, or feelings.
- Usually begins with "what if...", "if you...", or "what would...".
- Example: If you could accomplish all of your goals, what would your retirement look like?

Scaling Questions

- Typically an underutilized question form in financial planning.
- Useful to help clients gain an understanding of their progress towards their goals.
- Example: On a scale from 1 to 10, how anxious are you feeling about increasing your retirement savings?

13.5 DIRECTIVE VS. NONDIRECTIVE COMMUNICATION

Sometimes it will be appropriate to be directive in your verbal communication with clients; other times it will be more appropriate to be nondirective. Directive communication is planner centered, and nondirective communication is client centered (Grable and Goetz, 2017). Nondirective communication techniques are typically more useful when it comes to establishing the client relationship during the first few meetings. Once a trusting relationship has been established and the planning process moves to plan implementation, it will likely make sense to shift to directive communication techniques. Directive and nondirective communication techniques are listed below.

Directive Communication Techniques	Nondirective Communication Techniques
• Interpretation	• Clarification
• Reframing	• Summarization
• Explanation	• Reflection
• Advice	• Paraphrasing
• Suggestion	
• Urging	
• Confrontation	
• Ultimatum	

13.6 NONVERBAL COMMUNICATION

[A] Nonverbal Cues in Client Communication

Not only can we learn a lot from our clients' nonverbal communication cues, but we should also be cognizant of the fact that clients are evaluating our own nonverbal cues. Planners can use nonverbal cues with intention to ensure their desired messages are being received by the client. Figure 13.2 summarizes some best practices that planners can

Figure 13.2. Nonverbal Communication Best Practices

Eye Contact	Establish eye contact before you start the conversation.	
	Don't dart your eyes around, and don't look down. This gives the impression of confusion or lack of confidence.	
	Use the 50/70 rule -	Listening - maintain eye contact 70% of the time
		Speaking - maintain eye contact 50% of the time
	When you look away, look away slowly.	
	People are less likely to disclose information when eye contact is broken.	
Space	Consider your client's level of comfort when determining the appropriate amount of space to keep between yourself and the client.	
	Public Space	Typical when meeting new people
		>3 feet apart
	Social Space	Typical when you meet an acquaintance.
		Between 2.5-3 feet apart.
	Personal Space	Typical when talking to people you know and trust.
		About 2 feet apart.
	Intimate Space	Typical when communicating with someone you know extremely well.
		<2 feet apart.
Tone, Rate, and Volume	Tone, rate, and volume are indicators of underlying emotion.	
	Mirror the client's volume, pacing, and tone in most situations.	
	In more rare situations, you can change the mood or direction of the conversation by counteracting the client's pace and volume.	If the client is upset, agitated, or worked up, consider slowing your pace and lowering your volume to bring calm to an intense situation.
		If you need to send a message about your competence or give credence to your abilities, raising your volume and using a confident tone may be useful.
Using Formal Language	Adapt the formality of your words and phrases based on your client.	Women tend to prefer more formal language. Men tend to prefer more informal language.
Specifi- city	Different people may take away different messages from the words you say.	Women tend to focus on the exact and precise meaning of the words you choose.
		Men tend to focus on the overall or general meaning of the words or sentences used.
Nature of the Words Chosen	Choose your words carefully, especially when communicating with women.	Men tend to be indifferent to the level of hostility of a word.
		Women prefer less aggressive words and tones.

[B] Cultural Considerations in Nonverbal Communication

It is important to recognize that it can be difficult to deliver universal best practices related to nonverbal communication because different cultures have different acceptable or preferred communication practices. For example, eye contact is typically expected and encouraged in Western cultures. However, many Eastern cultures see eye contact as a sign of disrespect. John Grable and Joe Goetz (2017) have compiled a table of acceptable and unacceptable gestures and communication practices by culture in their book *Communication Essentials for Financial Planners: Strategies and Techniques* which may be a helpful reference to obtain a better understanding of culturally sensitive communication techniques.

13.7 ACTIVE LISTENING

Active listening is the process of listening with intention and actively engaging with the speaker. This is one of the most important skills for financial planners to learn when engaging with clients. Active listening goes far beyond *hearing* the client's words and being able to remember what the client said. Active listening provides a structure to use when truly trying to *listen* and understand the message the client is trying to impart. Active listening requires you to quiet your mind and mute your personal reactions to the words the client is saying. This allows you to give your full attention to your client, providing greater opportunity for building understanding and trust. See Figure 13.3 for characteristics of active listening.

When you are using active listening, it is important to be patient, let the client take the lead, pay attention to body language, ask well-timed questions, and know when to use the power of silence (Agency for Toxic Substances and Disease Registry [ATSDR], n.d.).

Figure 13.3. Active Listening Characteristics

A	Attitude

- Listen with an open mind.
- Listen with a positive attitude and limit negative thoughts.
- Make judgements about what was said AFTER the client has finished speaking.

A	Attention

- Be present and focus. Listen with intention.
- Mirror their body language. Show warmth in your facial expressions.
- Don't check out once you think you know what the client is going to say.

A	Adjustment

- Be flexible.
- Be open to changing your mind.
- Do not think about reacting or anticipating what the client is going to say.

Figure 13.4 summarizes some of the main strategies you can use when you are listening actively.

Figure 13.4. Active Listening Strategies

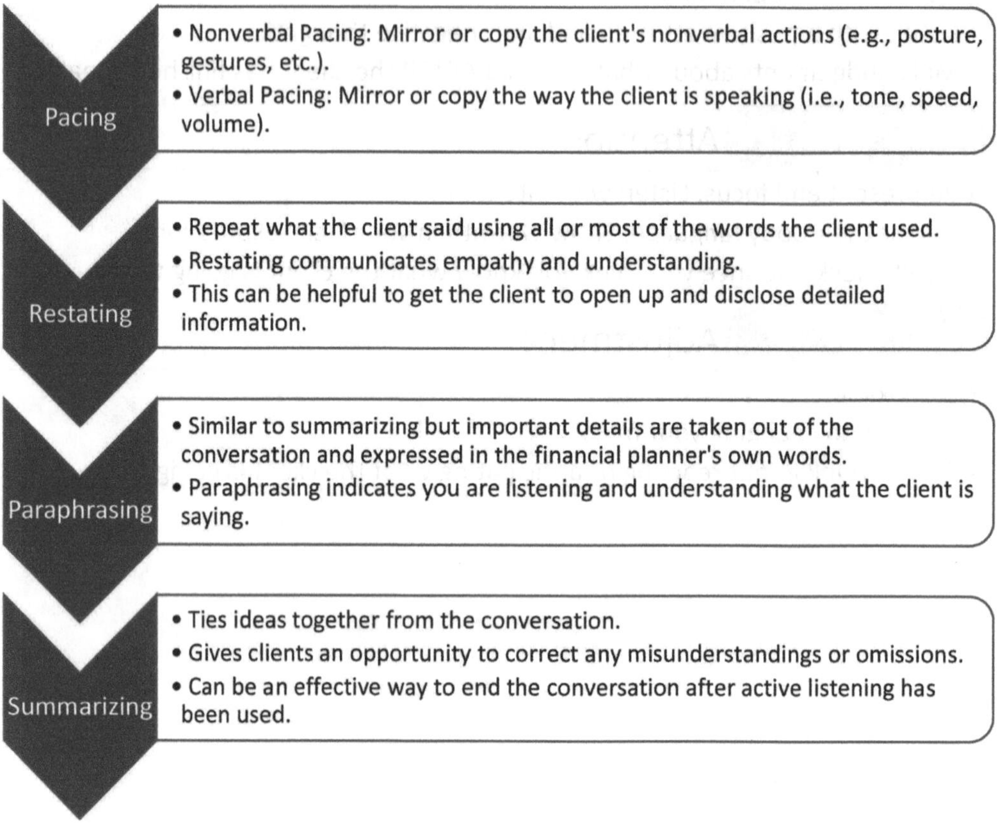

Pacing
- Nonverbal Pacing: Mirror or copy the client's nonverbal actions (e.g., posture, gestures, etc.).
- Verbal Pacing: Mirror or copy the way the client is speaking (i.e., tone, speed, volume).

Restating
- Repeat what the client said using all or most of the words the client used.
- Restating communicates empathy and understanding.
- This can be helpful to get the client to open up and disclose detailed information.

Paraphrasing
- Similar to summarizing but important details are taken out of the conversation and expressed in the financial planner's own words.
- Paraphrasing indicates you are listening and understanding what the client is saying.

Summarizing
- Ties ideas together from the conversation.
- Gives clients an opportunity to correct any misunderstandings or omissions.
- Can be an effective way to end the conversation after active listening has been used.

13.8 THE FLOW PROCESS

Brad and Ted Klontz developed a technique called The Flow Process which they teach in their Exquisite Listening™ workshops and trainings. The Flow Process provides a good framework when a client is providing you with new information or you are establishing a new client relationship. The Flow Process, illustrated in Figure 13.5 consists of 7 steps (Klontz and Klontz, 2016).

Figure 13.5. The Flow Process

1. Start the conversation with an invitation.

- Start the conversation with a question.
- Klontz and Klontz suggest asking, "I have some items I would like to cover in the meeting today, but before we start on my agenda, I am curious what concerns you most today."

2. Listen intently.

- Use active listening techniques.
- Consider physically moving the agenda and putting it to the side.

3. Summarize what you heard.

- Use summarizing techniques, especially if you feel the client's energy drop (the client pauses) or they seem to be talking in circles.
- The summary can be short. Sometimes just a few words are sufficient.

4. Ask if there is anything you have missed.

- Keep the phrasing of your question simple when you ask if anything was missed.
- "Tell me more about..."
- "I am curious about..."
- "I would like to know more about..."
- "Say more about..."

5. When the client's energy drops, repeat Steps 3 and 4.

- If their energy increases when you ask if there is anything you missed, continue to listen. If energy decreases, decide whether it is appropriate to move back to step 3 or forward to step 6.

6. Pick a word, phrase, idea, or concept and invite the speaker to give more information.

- You could ask, "tell me more about what financial security means to you" or "can you expand on what you mean when you say uncontrollable spending?"

7. End with a grand summary.

- Summarize the conversation in 3-4 sentences.
- At the end of the summary, ask again if you have missed anything. If they add to the narrative, summarize the new information once they have finished.

13.9 MULTIFACETED COMMUNICATION: DO'S AND DON'TS

The left-side column in the chart below identifies effective multifaceted communication methods. The column on the right contains steps that should be avoided as they can be detrimental in your pursuit of building a connection with your clients.

Do	Don't
• Do use visual aids (graphs, charts, figures, etc.) to assist with communicating recommendations if possible.	• Don't assume a typical meeting room layout with a large desk or table between the planner and the client is the least stressful layout for the client. Consider sitting in couches or chairs without a table between you.
• Do consider your client's cultural norms and values when communicating with them (i.e., spacing, shaking hands, eye contact, etc.).	• Don't assume every client will communicate in the same way or will be equally receptive to your preferred communication style and techniques.
• Do consider meeting with your clients in a controlled environment such as your office and reduce the physical barriers between yourself and the client	
• Do sit about an arm's length away from your client when sitting down for a meeting.	
• Do use a variety of verbal, nonverbal, and visual techniques to gather information about your clients and communicate your recommendations	

References

Agency for Toxic Substances and Disease Registry. (n.d.). *A guide to active listening*. Centers for Disease Control and Prevention. https://www.atsdr.cdc.gov/ceplaybook/docs/active-listening-guide-508.pdf.

Chatterjee, S. and Sages, R. (2022). Multifaceted communication. In S. Chatterjee, S. Lutter and D. Yeske (Eds.), *The Psychology of Financial Planning* (ch. 13). Certified Financial Planner Board of Standards, Inc.

Coghlan, A. T., Preskill, H. and Catsambas, T. T. (2003). An overview of appreciative inquiry in evaluation. In H. Preskill and A. T. Coghlan (Eds.), *Using appreciative inquiry in evaluation* (pp. 5–22). Jossey-Bass.

Gerbner, G. (1958). On content analysis and critical research in mass communication. *Audio Visual Communication Review*, 6(3), 85-108.

Grable, J. E. and Goetz, J. W. (2017). *Communication essentials for financial planners: Strategies and techniques*. John Wiley & Sons.

Klontz, B. and Klontz, T. (2016). 7 steps to facilitate exquisite listening. *Journal of Financial Planning*, 29(11), 24-26.

Chapter 14

Navigating Change

14.1 INTRODUCTION

Some financial planners find helping clients navigate the changes in their lives to be one of the most rewarding parts of financial planning. Nevertheless, it can be overwhelming and stressful when a client unexpectedly reveals they are going through a crisis event, and they turn to you for guidance and

Crisis
A situation where a person feels a situation is intolerable and that the situation demands more resources and coping mechanisms than they currently possess.

help. This chapter will focus on helping you to evaluate whether the change your client is going through constitutes a crisis event as well as providing some practical tips to help you take care of yourself so that you can best serve your clients going through these situations.

Not every challenging situation a client faces necessarily constitutes a crisis. A crisis is a situation where a person feels a situation is intolerable and that the situation demands more resources and coping mechanisms than they currently possess (James and Gilliland, 2016). The key component of this definition is insufficient resources to deal with the situation at hand. You can help clients in crisis by helping them to identify the resources they do have available and by connecting them with some additional resources that can help them cope with the crisis.

Dubofsky and Sussman (2009) compiled a list of non-financial issues that clients brought up with the financial planners they surveyed. Around 64% of financial planners had experienced the most frequent non-financial issue (personal life goals) and about 5% had experienced the most infrequent non-financial issue (sexual problems). Below is a summary of these non-financial issues that financial planners could encounter in their practice which could escalate to a crisis:

- Personal life goals

- Physical health

- Job / Career / Profession

- The death of someone close

- Conflict with children

- Marital problems

- Children's medical / emotional problems

- Divorce

- Conflicts with extended family

- Spending addiction

- Legal problems

- Religious / spiritual issues

- Mental health

- Depression / General unhappiness

- Children's addiction

- Client's addictions

- Sexual problems

14.2 NAVIGATING CHANGE IN PRACTICE

Some of the common change situations that financial planners may see in their practice include, death, disability, divorce, the birth of a child or grandchild, an adoption, a career change, or the unexpected loss of a job. Just because a client may be prepared for some or all of these events financially does not mean they will have a stress-free or emotionless experience.

The list below highlights some of the most important concepts from Chapter 14: Navigating Change in *The Psychology of Financial Planning* (Lutter et al., 2022) that may be particularly relevant to you in your financial planning practice.

- Take your time in assessing your client's level of stress during periods of change in their lives. Your first priority should be to listen actively to fully understand the ramifications of the change.

- Based on what you learn from the client, carefully consider the circumstances and the appropriate role for you in the situation.

- If the situation is primarily a high stress situation, help your client to understand the circumstances they are facing and fully explore their feelings about the situation. Once this has been established, you can pivot to brainstorming solutions or providing financial advice, if appropriate and relevant.

- If the situation goes beyond a stressor or stressful situation and is best classified as a crisis, consider whether a referral or a partnership with a financial therapist or other mental health professional is most appropriate for the client.

- You are certain to encounter a number of clients going through crisis situations. During difficult economic times, you may have a high volume of clients experiencing stress. Make sure you are available and capable of serving your clients by practicing self-care actively and with regularity.

14.3 HOW TO RECOGNIZE A CRISIS AND DECIDE WHETHER A REFERRAL IS APPROPRIATE

Due to the nature of the financial planning profession, you will certainly encounter clients in crisis. However, as mentioned previously, not every difficult situation a client faces is necessarily a crisis. Family Stress Theory provides a good framework to understand what constitutes a crisis and the factors that can magnify a crisis. Figure 14.1 details the three factors, A factor, B factor, and C factor, that each combine to influence how much stress will ultimately be experienced, the X factor.

Figure 14.1. Family Stress Theory

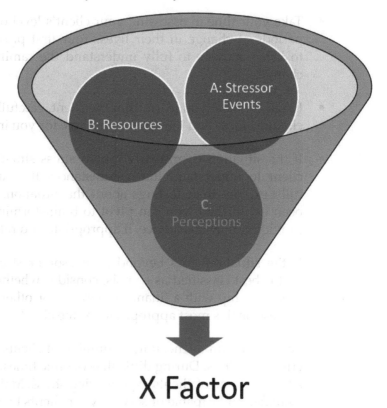

A crisis occurs when each of the three factors listed in the figure above overwhelm the client. Once the client no longer has resources to deal with the stress and stressor event, a crisis occurs. However, how the client perceives their resources and the severity of the crisis can be more important than reality. For example, a client may perceive they have fewer resources than they actually do and, consequently, may act impulsively to avoid a perceived crisis. You can help your client if you feel their perception of the crisis or their perception of the resources they have available are misaligned with reality.

Figure 14.2 describes the responses that clients may encounter in the face of a crisis. The figure also summarizes some indicators that you can use to identify which stress response your client may be experiencing.

Figure 14.2. Crisis Responses

Flight	Fight	Freeze
• Avoiding • Missed appointments • Ignored calls and emails • Checking phone	• Anger • Blame • Disagreement with recommendations	• Confusion • Ambivalence • Cold or numb • Restricted breathing • No questions

14.4 HELPING A CLIENT IN CRISIS

When clients are truly in crisis, it is important to help them identify the resources they have available to them during the crisis. If clients are experiencing heightened stress or excess physiological arousal, they may not be able to think clearly about their next steps or the resources available to them. Once you've identified the resources already available to the client, you can help them identify where the shortfalls might be and develop a plan to acquire additional resources to overcome the crisis (see Figure 14.3).

Figure 14.3. Financial Resilience

Financial Resilience

Human Capital	Social Capital	Financial Capital
• Education • Training • Certifications • Experience • Intelligence • Willingness to Relocate	• Social Networks • Community Engagement • Social Identity • Relationship Reciprocity	• Insurance • Real Property • Cash • Financial Accounts

Figure 14.4 can be used as a four-step guide to help clients who are currently undergoing a crisis. The first thing you should do when a client comes to you with a crisis is to assess the situation. Primarily, this stage involves listening to the client. Second, you can work with the client to identify the most significant concerns. Once you understand the situation and the main problems at hand, you can do what you can to help by slowing any potential long-term damage the crisis may cause the client. Lastly, you can help the client get specialized, advanced assistance if you are not trained and/or licensed to provide the necessary help required.

Figure 14.4. Guide to Handling a Crisis

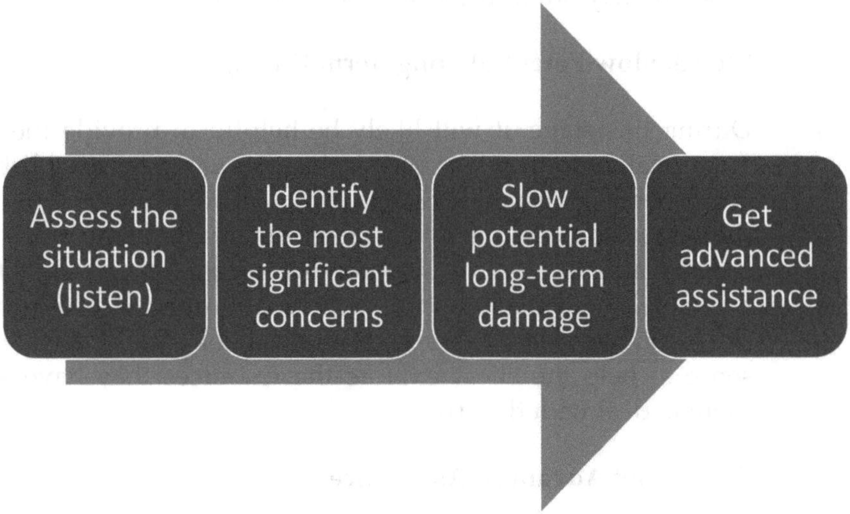

Step 1. Assess the Situation

In this stage, you can use the following skills and techniques to assess the client's situation. During this part of the process, you need to identify what crisis the client is experiencing and gather the relevant data. Be genuine and sincere with your concern during this step of the process. Active listening and empathy are essential skills to practice during this step of the process.

Active Listening. Use active listening techniques to ensure you are truly understanding the client's situation. See Chapter 13 for detailed instructions about how to utilize active listening techniques.

Empathy. Be empathetic and authentic as you listen and respond to a client in crisis. See Chapter 15 for techniques you can use with your clients to demonstrate empathy and build your empathetic muscles.

Step 2. Identify the Most Significant Concerns

The next step involves identifying the most significant concerns for the client. Of course, making sure the client is safe should be the main priority. Once the client's safety has been established, you can move to providing support. The goal here is not to "fix" the problem. The

some intentional work together with the client as the largest parts of the problem may not immediately be apparent.

Step 3. Slow Potential Long-Term Damage

During this stage, it will likely be helpful to provide the client with emotional support. Once physical safety has been established, ensure your client feels established as a person of value and communicate with them that you care. Help the client determine what courses of action are available to them or whether any alternative courses of action are available. In all likelihood, it will be appropriate to use many of the skills you have learned throughout this book. At this stage, it will make sense to help the client explore the resources they have available to them to deal with the crisis.

Step 4. Get Advanced Assistance

Much of crisis and intervention work is beyond the scope of practice of a financial planner. Encourage your client to seek help from appropriate mental health professionals and other trained practitioners that are trained to help during times of crisis. You should work to develop a referral network so that you are prepared before your clients face crises.

Developing a Referral Network. The first step in developing a referral network is to do your research. You should start building your referral network before you encounter a client in crisis. You will be grateful to have a referral network already in place once you need it. To start the process, begin evaluating the professional qualifications of the mental health professionals and counselors that work in physical proximity to most of your clients. It also makes sense to start evaluating professionals that will provide services remotely or online. Some clients will, of course, prefer to meet with professionals in person while some will be comfortable or even prefer the flexibility of meeting remotely.

You can start with an internet search of the professionals you would like to include in your referral network (e.g., marriage and family therapists, financial therapists, individual therapists, sex therapists, financial coaches, etc.). Most professionals have developed a specialized subset of skills that will be most effective in specific client circumstances. You can use the Financial Therapy Associations' tool for "Find a Financial

Therapist" to find professionals that may suit a wide array of client needs. Approach this search as you would if you wanted to add a CPA or an estate planning attorney to your referral network. Foundationally, you need to evaluate whether they have the appropriate educational and licensing credentials. Once that has been established, you need to determine how they work with people. Do they have any online reviews? Has anyone in your personal or professional network worked with this person or this firm previously?

Once you've narrowed down the group to a manageable list of professionals with appropriate qualifications and a solid reputation, try to meet with them in person or virtually. Seek to understand their ideal client and the clients they can best serve in their practice.

Meanwhile, start collecting data about your client's preexisting mental health practitioners and counselors at client intake or during the data gathering process (Coambs, 2022). This will help you skip a step later if you need to get in touch with your client's other mental health professionals. Additionally, it will help you build your network of mental health professionals in your area or who provide services to people who are similar to your clients.

Once you find yourself in a situation where you need to make the referral to a client that does not have a mental health professional, you need to take care having that conversation with your client. The ideal scenario would involve the client acknowledging the problem themselves. Another situation where it may make sense to involve a mental health professional if there is a clear pattern of behavior beyond your scope of practice (i.e., drug abuse). Ed Coambs (2022) suggests that the conversation with a client becomes easier if they are willing to acknowledge a pattern. Ed suggests you ask a question like "I'm starting to notice this pattern. Are you seeing it? How much concern or distress is it causing you?" If the client can acknowledge the pattern and are frustrated by the pattern, you can more easily ask whether they would be interested in working with a mental health professional to address the deeper issues at play.

14.5 SELF-CARE IS ESSENTIAL

During stressful times, many advisors forget to practice self-care. As airlines are fond of reminding us, when it comes to oxygen mask deployment, you cannot help others if you yourself are incapacitated. So why is it that so many advisors find it so difficult to practice self-care?

In all likelihood, you already know the basics of self-care. Make sure you are getting enough sleep and have a regular sleep schedule. Eat a healthy and balanced diet. Try to build exercise into your daily routine. These steps are very important, but there are also other steps you can take. Meghaan Lurtz (2020) recommends the following steps:

1. Have a designated stop time.

2. Indicate your stop and start time to others.

3. Create white space (i.e., give yourself breaks between meetings and time when you can reset).

4. Hold a webinar if you need to communicate something to a large number of clients instead of having separate individual meetings with each client).

5. Let it out (i.e., talk with people and stay connected, make sure you have a good support system in place).

Compassion fatigue and burnout are relatively common in the financial advisor community. Compassion fatigue can happen when financial planners take on the stress, trauma, or the suffering of their clients (Clay, 2020). This can occur from over-empathizing and not creating strong boundaries. Develop a self-care routine. Examine your beliefs about self-care. Self-care is a necessity and it should be encouraged and celebrated. Be compassionate with yourself just as you are with your clients. Lean on your community, at work and at home. It is important to feel connected to people. When possible, help your colleagues. Trying to spread out the workload when one person or a few members of the team are particularly busy can help. They will probably be willing to help you when you're the one with a heavy workload, especially if this practice becomes ingrained in your firm culture.

14.6 NAVIGATING CHANGE: DO'S AND DON'TS

The list below summarizes some of the key steps financial planners can take to navigate change. The column on the right contains steps that should be avoided as they can be detrimental in your pursuit of building a connection with your client.

Do	Don't
• Practice self-care intentionally and with regularity. Make self-care a habit.	• Don't try to be your client's therapist.
• Do know how to recognize a crisis and differentiate it from stress or a stressor.	• Don't practice outside your scope of skills. Know when to make a referral.
• Do practice your empathy skills to help clients in crisis (see Chapter 15).	• Don't let a lack of your own self-awareness create additional stress for your client.
• Do help your clients build their financial resiliency so they are better equipped to deal with financial stressors.	
• Do acknowledge the non-financial components of the crisis in addition to the financial components.	
• Do provide your clients with a supportive environment to discuss and work through issues. This may help free up cognitive-processing ability to deal with the effects of the crisis.	

References

Clay, R. A. (2020, June 11). *Are you experiencing compassion fatigue?* American Psychological Association. https://www.apa.org/topics/covid-19/compassion-fatigue.

Coambs, E. (2022, February 15). *Best practices for introducing financial therapy to clients in need.* eMoney. https://emoneyadvisor.com/blog/best-practices-for-introducing-financial-therapy-to-clients-in-need/.

Dubofsky, D. and Sussman, L. (2009). The changing role of the financial planner part 1: From financial analytics to coaching and life planning. *Journal of Financial Planning*, 22(8), 48-57.

James, R. K. and Gilliland, B. E. (2016). *Crisis intervention strategies.* Cengage Learning.

Lurtz, M. (2020, March 18). Self-care and self-compassion in times of financial stress and anxiety. *Kitces.com.* https://www.kitces.com/blog/advisor-client-self-care-self-compassion-financial-anxiety-traumatic-stress-ptsd/.

Lutter, S., McCoy, M., Davis, S. and Palmer, L. (2022). Navigating change. In S. Chatterjee, S. Lutter and D. Yeske (Eds.), *The Psychology of Financial Planning* (ch. 14). Certified Financial Planner Board of Standards, Inc.

Chapter 15

Building Your Empathetic Muscles

15.1 INTRODUCTION

Before discussing how to grow your empathetic ability, it's important to define empathy. As defined in *The Psychology of Financial Planning*, empathy is "the ability to feel what someone is feeling and to fully imagine what it is like to walk in their shoes. Empathy is hearing and communicating with full attention, professionalism, and unbiased reaction" (McCoy and Lutter, 2022). An important part of empathy is trying to understand what someone else is going through, but it can also extend to taking action by trying to understand what might help (Saxey, 2020).

15.2 EMPATHY IN PRACTICE

Empathy in a financial planning practice can take many forms. Emotional empathy involves feeling the pain of another and trying to alleviate their pain and your own resulting discomfort. Emotional empathy can result in experiencing the same emotions as someone else.

Emotional Empathy

Emotional empathy involves feeling the pain of another and trying to alleviate their pain and your own resulting discomfort. Emotional empathy can result in experiencing the same emotions as someone else. Emotional empathy is typically most effective with individuals we feel are similar to ourselves.

Emotional empathy is typically most effective with individuals we feel are similar to ourselves (Lurtz, 2021). Cognitive empathy is understanding the level and significance of some else's emotional experience. It involves helping someone cope with their distress and doesn't necessarily mean trying to take their pain away (Lurtz, 2021).

Of course, you should demonstrate empathy towards your clients as this can help to build deeper connections and more meaningful relationships with them. But empathy should also extend to your co-workers and/or your employees and even towards yourself. You can practice self-empathy by being kind towards yourself. Remember, you are an essential part of the client-practitioner relationship, and you cannot serve your clients to the best of your ability if you are physically and emotionally worn out.

Below are some important concepts from Chapter 15: The Necessity of Empathy in *The Psychology of Financial Planning* (McCoy and Lutter, 2022) that are particularly relevant to financial planning practitioners.

- Empathy is like a muscle. If you would like to increase your empathy, you must intentionally build and exercise your empathy. Much of this chapter is designed to help you grow your empathy with helpful tips and useful exercises.

- Sympathy is much easier to demonstrate than empathy. If you think empathy is as easy as saying "I understand how you feel," you still have a lot of work to do.

> **Cognitive Empathy**
>
> Cognitive empathy is understanding the level and significance of some else's emotional experience. It involves helping someone cope with their distress and doesn't necessarily mean trying to take their pain away.

- Empathy is professional.

- Empathy may decrease the longer you practice. It is important to intentionally practice empathy over the course of your career, and you may need to increase your efforts over time.

- Self-care when practicing empathy is essential to avoid emotional burnout. One way to avoid emotional burnout is to focus on cognitive empathy in addition to emotional empathy. It may be helpful to set emotional boundaries for yourself by recognizing you can be empathetic and build a personal connection with someone without taking personal emotional responsibility for their situation.

15.3 ARE YOU EMPATHETIC OR JUST SYMPATHETIC?

If you are trying to build your empathetic muscles, it is important to be able to distinguish empathy from sympathy. Sympathy simply means feeling sorry for someone (McCoy and Lutter, 2022).

Empathy goes far beyond sympathy. As Brené Brown (2013) puts it, "Empathy fuels connection. Sympathy drives disconnection." Empathy is the opposite of shame (Brown, 2006). This is particularly important when clients come to you for help when they feel they've made financial mistakes or have mismanaged their finances. They may feel shame about their circumstances, and empathy will be an important part of helping them to open up and be honest about their circumstances.

15.4 ASSESS YOUR EMPATHY

Empathy is a construct that is quite difficult to measure. When people are asked about specific situations and how they would react in terms of empathy, it can be very difficult to know and represent accurately. The Interpersonal Reactivity Index has become a popular index to assess dispositional empathy which is empathy that is considered to be a stable character trait (Davis, 1983). The scale contains four different sub-scales: the perspective-taking scale (PT), the fantasy scale (FS), the empathic concern scale (EC), and the personal distress scale (PD). The questions and how to score each question are laid out in Figure 15.1.

Figure 15.1. Interpersonal Reactivity Index

		Does Not Describe Me Well				Describes Me Very Well
1.	I daydream and fantasize, with some regularity, about things that might happen to me. (FS)	0	1	2	3	4
2.	I often have tender, concerned feelings for people less fortunate than me. (EC)	0	1	2	3	4
3.	I sometimes find it difficult to see things from the "other guy's" point of view. (PT)	4	3	2	1	0
4.	Sometimes I don't feel very sorry for other people when they are having problems. (EC)	4	3	2	1	0
5.	I really get involved with the feelings of the characters in a novel. (FS)	0	1	2	3	4
6.	In emergency situations, I feel apprehensive and ill-at-ease. (PD)	0	1	2	3	4
7.	I am usually objective when I watch a movie or play, and I don't often get completely caught up in it. (FS)	4	3	2	1	0
8.	I try to look at everybody's side of a disagreement before I make a decision. (PT)	0	1	2	3	4
9.	When I see someone being taken advantage of, I feel kind of protective towards them. (EC)	0	1	2	3	4
10.	I sometimes feel helpless when I am in the middle of a very emotional situation. (PD)	0	1	2	3	4
11.	I sometimes try to understand my friends better by imagining how things look from their perspective. (PT)	0	1	2	3	4
12.	Becoming extremely involved in a good book or movie is somewhat rare for me. (FS)	4	3	2	1	0
13.	When I see someone get hurt, I tend to remain calm. (PD)	4	3	2	1	0
14.	Other people's misfortunes do not usually disturb me a great deal.	4	3	2	1	0
15.	If I'm sure I'm right about something, I don't waste much time listening to other people's arguments. (PT)	4	3	2	1	0
16.	After seeing a play or movie, I have felt as though I were one of the characters. (FS)	0	1	2	3	4
17.	Being in a tense emotional situation scares me. (PD)	0	1	2	3	4
18.	When I see someone being treated unfairly, I sometimes don't feel very much pity for them. (EC)	4	3	2	1	0

		Does Not Describe Me Well				Describes Me Very Well
19.	I am usually pretty effective in dealing with emergencies. (PD)	4	3	2	1	0
20.	I am often quite touched by things that I see happen. (EC)	0	1	2	3	4
21.	I believe that there are two sides to every question and try to look at them both. (PT)	0	1	2	3	4
22.	I would describe myself as a pretty soft-hearted person. (EC)	0	1	2	3	4
23.	When I watch a good movie, I can very easily put myself in the place of a leading character. (FS)	0	1	2	3	4
24.	I tend to lose control during emergencies. (PD)	0	1	2	3	4
25.	When I'm upset at someone, I usually try to "put myself in his shoes" for a while. (PT)	0	1	2	3	4
26.	When I am reading an interesting story or novel, I imagine how I would feel if the events in the story were happening to me. (FS)	0	1	2	3	4
27.	When I see someone who badly needs help in an emergency, I go to pieces. (PD)	0	1	2	3	4
28.	Before criticizing somebody, I try to imagine how I would feel if I were in their place. (PT)	0	1	2	3	4

15.5 BUILDING EMPATHY

The mnemonic device in Figure 15.2 (Riess and Kraft-Todd, 2014) can help you remember the important components of communicating empathy. Each box contains practical tips that you can implement in your client meetings and daily life.

Figure 15.2. Communicating Empathy

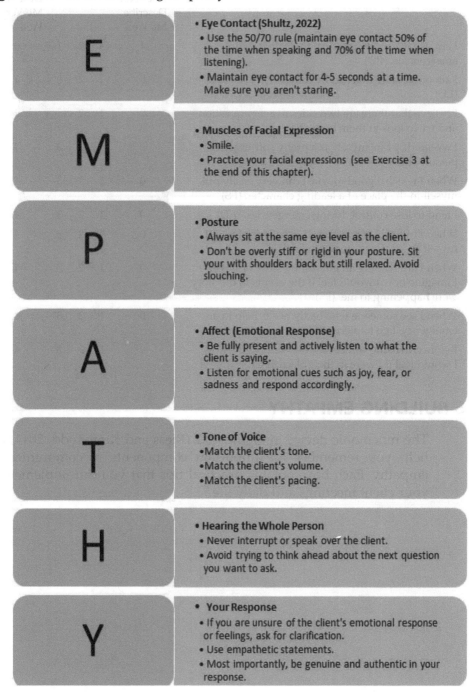

E
- **Eye Contact (Shultz, 2022)**
  - Use the 50/70 rule (maintain eye contact 50% of the time when speaking and 70% of the time when listening).
  - Maintain eye contact for 4-5 seconds at a time. Make sure you aren't staring.

M
- **Muscles of Facial Expression**
  - Smile.
  - Practice your facial expressions (see Exercise 3 at the end of this chapter).

P
- **Posture**
  - Always sit at the same eye level as the client.
  - Don't be overly stiff or rigid in your posture. Sit your with shoulders back but still relaxed. Avoid slouching.

A
- **Affect (Emotional Response)**
  - Be fully present and actively listen to what the client is saying.
  - Listen for emotional cues such as joy, fear, or sadness and respond accordingly.

T
- **Tone of Voice**
  - Match the client's tone.
  - Match the client's volume.
  - Match the client's pacing.

H
- **Hearing the Whole Person**
  - Never interrupt or speak over the client.
  - Avoid trying to think ahead about the next question you want to ask.

Y
- **Your Response**
  - If you are unsure of the client's emotional response or feelings, ask for clarification.
  - Use empathetic statements.
  - Most importantly, be genuine and authentic in your response.

15.6 EMPATHETIC STATEMENTS FOR FINANCIAL PLANNING PRACTITIONERS

Empathetic statements can take a lot of different forms. When being empathetic, one of the most important outcomes is building a connection (Brown, 2013). Try out some of the phrases below in your conversations at home and the office. Some of these phrases may feel more natural to you than others. Remember, authenticity is essential to empathy and building a connection, so don't use empathetic phrases that don't feel like something *you* would say. Feel free to adapt these phrases to your own personal voice.

- I understand what you are saying.

- I support your position.

- That would have upset me too!

- That sounds really exciting!

- Although I'm not quite sure what to say right now, I'm really glad you told me about this (Saxey, 2020).

- I have no idea what that must be like for you.

- Thank you for opening up to me. I know this must be hard to talk about.

- Is there anything else you want to share?

- That sounds really challenging.

- I can see why you feel that way, but I feel differently because…. (Imbs, 2020)

15.7 EMPATHY: DO'S AND DON'TS

The list below summarizes some of the key steps financial planners can take to promote empathy. The column on the right contains steps that should be avoided as they can be detrimental in your pursuit of

Do	Don't
• Do smile (when appropriate).	• Don't assume you understand exactly how the other person feels.
• Do seek to understand their perspective.	• Don't use "look on the bright side" or "at least" statements.
• Do validate and normalize (when appropriate) their feelings.	• Don't offer unsolicited advice or use "you should…" statements.
• Do open up the conversation by asking clarifying questions.	• Don't be judgemental.
• Do put away your cellphone and any other devices to avoid distractions and demonstrate active listening.	• Don't overreact or make a snap decision on behalf of your client based on your emotional empathetic response.
• Do use the client's name (Loehr, 2016).	• Don't interrupt; jot down questions or comments on meeting materials to ask later.
• Do use genuine and authentic responses, even if it means admitting you don't know or don't understand (Loehr, 2016).	• Don't expect perfect communication from yourself or your clients.

15.8 PRACTICING EMPATHY

If empathy is a skill that does not feel natural to you, there are some steps you can take to practice your empathy muscles. Some exercises are listed below that you can use to assess your knowledge of empathy and practice your empathy skills.

#1 Identify each of the following statements as either sympathetic or empathetic responses:

1. I'm so sorry that happened to you. I just feel terrible for you.

   _____

2. I hear your concern about your daughter's ability to financially afford going to college, and I understand that it is weighing on you

#2 Financial Planning Case Study

Claire and Brad are currently facing some financial difficulties. After a series of unexpected expenditures, the newly married couple has found themselves in a less than ideal financial situation. To add to their predicament, their careers are not as advancing as quickly as they would have liked and any raises do not seem to be on the horizon. Because of this, much of their vision of the future regarding buying a house, having kids, and various vacations is being put on hold. All of these sudden financial hardships and mishaps are starting to add a substantial strain on their marriage. They are currently desperate for help.

Write down 2-3 examples of sympathetic statements you could use in this case. Now write 2-3 examples of empathetic statements. How are the empathetic statements different from the sympathetic statements? Did you use different words or phrases? How might the outcomes of using the empathetic statements differ from the outcomes of using the sympathetic statements?

#3 Empathy Exercises

Do you have good self-awareness of your facial expressions? In front of a mirror, remember a time that you were trying to sympathize or empathize with a client. Try to recreate the expression you would probably use if that situation occurred again. Is your face conveying the message you were trying to send? Take a photo of your expression and discuss with a trusted friend or colleague whether your expression is conveying the message you are trying to send.

If you typically have client meetings with other colleagues, ask them to give you feedback on your facial expression, posture, and other nonverbal cues during a meeting. They may be able to help you identify if you are sending unintended messages and provide suggestions as to how you can improve.

References

Brown, B. (2006). Shame resilience theory: A grounded theory study on women and shame. *Families in Society, 87*(1), 43-52.

Brown, B. (2013, December 10). *Brené Brown on empathy* [Video]. YouTube. https://www.youtube.com/watch?v=1Evwgu369Iw

Davis, M. H. (1983). Measuring individual differences in empathy: Evidence for a multidimensional approach. *Journal of Personality and Social Psychology, 44*(1), 113-126.

Imbs, N. S. (2020, March 31). *The value of empathy in the workplace*. American Society of Administrative Professionals. https://www.asaporg.com/the-value-of-empathy-in-the-workplace.

Loehr, A. (2016, May 6). 7 Practical tips for increasing empathy. *Huffpost*. https://www.huffpost.com/entry/seven-practical-tips-for-_b_9854350.

Lurtz, M. (2021). When more advisor empathy isn't better and the compassion-based alternative. *Kitces.com*. https://www.kitces.com/blog/against-emotional-cognitive-empathy-paul-bloom-financial-advisor-compassion-burnout/.

McCoy, M. and Lutter, S. (2022). The necessity of empathy. In S. Chatterjee, S. Lutter and D. Yeske (Eds.), *The Psychology of Financial Planning* (ch. 15). Certified Financial Planner Board of Standards, Inc.

Riess, H. and Kraft-Todd, G. (2014). E.M.P.A.T.H.Y.: A tool to enhance nonverbal communication between clinicians and their patients. *Academic Medicine, 89*(8), 1108-1112.

Saxey, M. (2020). Empathy v. sympathy: Are my attempts really helping others? *Family Perspectives, 2*(1), 1-3.

Schulz, J. (2012, December 31). *Eye contact: Don't make these mistakes*. MSU Extension. https://www.canr.msu.edu/news/eye_contact_dont_make_these_mistakes#:~:text=Use%20the%2050%2F70%20rule,it%20for%204%2D5%20seconds.

Index